Reading Explorers

A Guided Skills-Based Journey

Year 5

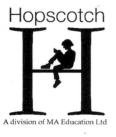

Hopscotch

A division of MA Education Ltd

John Murray

Hopscotch

A division of MA Education Ltd

Published by
Hopscotch, a division of MA Education,
St Jude's Church, Dulwich Road,
London, SE24 0PB
www.hopscotchbooks.com
020 7738 5454

© 2009 MA Education Ltd.

Written by John Murray

Illustrated by Emma Squire, Fonthill Creative, 01722 717057

ISBN 978 1 90539 060 1

Every effort has been made to trace the owners of
copyright of material in this book and the publisher
apologises for any inadvertent omissions. Any persons
claiming copyright for any material should contact the
publisher who will be happy to pay the permission fees
agreed between them and who will amend the information
in this book on any subsequent reprint.

Extract from The New Oxford School Dictionary (OUP, 2007)
reprinted by permission of Oxford University Press.

Extract from The Iron Man by Ted Hughes by kind
permission of Faber & Faber Children's Books.

Contents Page

Introduction

About this series

Reading Explorers – A Guided Skills-Based Programme is a self-contained programme of work which has been developed to enhance the teaching and learning of guided reading.

It aims to provide teachers with a scheme of work that will enhance the development and continuity of guided reading throughout the school. More importantly, the programme actively promotes the teaching and learning of specific reading and study skills. The children thus acquire the ability to access, interpret and understand a piece of text, and are encouraged to become more independent thinkers and learners.

The main reason for the programme's success is that it is a skills-based programme which fulfils the needs of the developing learner. The pupils themselves are aware of the specific skills they are hoping to achieve each half term and are actively involved in developing these skills through the use of wipe board and kinaesthetic activities. They are also taught how to analyse the question being asked before they attempt to look for an answer. With this approach, teachers can support the children as they become independent learners in a structured and progressive manner.

The five thinking and reasoning skills contained in this programme are as follows:

Literal thinking
Deductive reasoning
Inferential skills
Evaluative assessment of texts
Study skills which promote wider independent study

There are five books in the series, one book per year group from Year 2 to Year 6, each with an accompanying CD-ROM.

Year 2 (Ages 6-7)

Year 3 (Ages 7-8)

Year 4 (Ages 8-9)

Year 5 (Ages 9-10)

Year 6 (Ages 10-11)

Each book and CD-ROM aims to:

- support teachers by providing a programme of work that covers enough lessons for a whole year
- reduce teachers' preparation time through the provision of differentiated activities and resources
- develop children's comprehension skills through purposeful and stimulating activities
- provide children with the opportunity to access a range of different texts and genres.

About this book

This book is for teachers of children in Year 5 and includes the following:

- A planning matrix of the skills to be taught throughout the series.
- A contents page that gives an overview of which skill a particular text is encouraging.
- Six detailed lesson plans with accompanying photocopiable texts for each half term (36 in total)
- A CD-ROM that is compatible with interactive white boards.

The CD-ROM

This provides differentiated text for each lesson plan. It also contains supporting resource materials which will prove useful when delivering each lesson.

The main text in each book is aimed at the average reading ability of the children of this age range. The texts provided on the CD-ROM are at a level below and a level above the texts in the book. This will allow all children within the classroom setting to access both the text and the specific reading or study skill being taught during each half term.

The planning matrix

A planning matrix is provided immediately after the sample lesson plan. Each ✓ symbol represents how often a particular skill should be taught during each academic year. Each ✓ symbol = 1 half term lasting approximately 6 weeks.

The contents page

Once a skill has been chosen to teach, the teacher can then choose an appropriate lesson within the specific reading skill. As the lessons within each skill are self-contained, they can be undertaken in any order.

Lesson plans

The book contains 36 lessons – enough for six per half term. The heading of each section indicates the specific skill to be taught and practised in each lesson. The lesson plans are divided into four sections:

■ Warm up questions
This part should be carried out first. The questions are usually literal, their purpose being to orientate the children with the text provided.

■ Main questions
This is the main body of the lesson and the types of questions posed here relate directly to the skill being practised.

The same questions can be used with all three texts for each lesson and, where appropriate, the answers are provided in brackets.

■ Essential Vocabulary
These questions or activities support the Main Questions section. They increase children's knowledge and understanding of words and help promote an understanding of why certain words were chosen by the author.

■ Evaluative questions
This section does more than simply help the teacher to round off the lesson. It allows children to speculate on the tone and purpose of the text, as well as to consider the text's audience. It also enables teachers to ask further questions on the social relevance a text may have in today's society.

Important information to read before carrying out the lesson plans

How to prepare and carry out the lessons

You will need:

- A wipe board and pen
- Any prompt cards associated with your learning aim (see below)

The children will need:

- A wipe board and pen
- A photocopy of the reading text
- A highlighter pen

Introducing the session to the children

First, settle your reading group and make sure each child has a wipe board, a dry marker and a highlighter pen. It is important that the children know which reading or study skill they are focusing on throughout each half term. Specific learning objectives should be discussed with the children at the beginning of each half term and you can remind them of these at the beginning of each session. A model is provided below:

- Who can tell me what type of questions we are focusing on this half term?

  - *Deductive*

- Good. (The teacher now sticks the deductive symbol* on the board) And what did we say the word deductive sounds like?

  - *Detective*

- Well done. So as a detective, what do we have to look for?

  - *Evidence, clues, proof*

- And where will we find this evidence?

  - *We can highlight words or sentences on our sheet.*

- Well remembered. I think you've earned your detective badge now and we can begin. (The teacher now gives each child their own pre-prepared detective badge* to wear during the lesson).

It is important to write the children's answers up so they can be clearly seen throughout your lesson. This will act as a visual reminder to each child of what their learning intention is – not simply for this lesson but for the whole half term.

Below are examples of the symbols you may wish to use to represent each skill. Over time, the children will recognise and associate each symbol with its relevant skill, especially if the same symbols are used throughout the school.

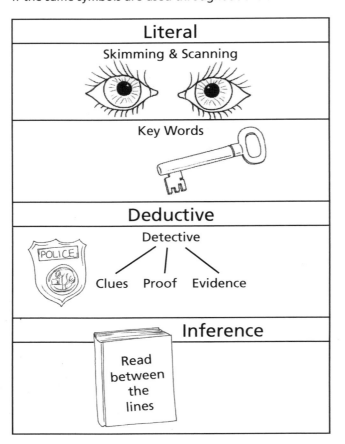

Icons included on the CD

Prior to reading the text

Provide the children with a copy of the text and ask them to scan the page to look for clues which tell them what type of text it is. Is it fiction or non-fiction? What genre of text is it? How can they tell this?

What do they think the text might contain? Ask them to look at the illustrations, title, headings, sub-headings and layout to give them clues. Can they predict what the text will be about? What do they already know about this particular genre?

Ask the children to quietly read through the text to familiarise themselves with it. They can circle any unfamiliar words they encounter. Any words circled can be discussed as a group and, later on, be put into the children's personal dictionaries. These can either be used to provide vocabulary extension work for particular groups or can provide extra words for their weekly spellings.

The warm up questions (3-5 minutes)

Next, ask the questions contained in the 'warm up' part of the lesson plan. This will give the children a purpose for their reading of the text and will enable them to search for specific information as they read. By doing this, the children will orientate themselves with the text provided and be able to use their past experiences to make predictions as to what else the text might consider.

Share the children's answers to the warm up questions. In which part of the text did they find their answers to the questions? Which parts of the text helped them find their answer more quickly? (Encourage the children to use correct terminology such as 'heading', 'first paragraph', 'caption', 'illustration' and 'column'.) Were the children's predictions about the text correct? Were they surprised by the text in any way?

The main questions (15-20 minutes)

During this part of the lesson you will be concentrating on the key skill or question type chosen for your half term focus. For this reason it is important that you give a weighty amount of time to looking at each question.

To determine that the children have understood the question and feel confident enough to start looking for the answer, the following approach can be taken:

A 5-staged helping hand approach

1. Ask the children to turn over their text so that they cannot see it.

2. Write out the question you want to ask on your wipe board and show the children. Ask them to read it and write the most important words or phrases onto their wipe board. When the group has finished, ask them to show each other their answers.

    For example, you might write 'What is the name of Captain Teller's space ship?" The children would read this and write down the key words 'name' and 'ship'.

3. Discuss how relevant the chosen key words are when searching for the answer and where they might find the answer in the text itself. As the children begin to understand that there may be more than one key word in a question, discussion may also take place as to which key word should take precedence over another.

4. Ask the children to turn over their text and begin looking for the answer. Once they have found it they should highlight it on the text and write down the answer on their wipe board.

5. When everyone has finished, ask individuals to reveal their answer by showing their wipe board to the group. Answers can then be discussed accordingly and additional evidence highlighted on the text itself.

Evaluative questions (3-5 minutes)

These questions round the session off and enable the children to reflect on the tone, purpose and overall effectiveness of the text. Exploring these questions will also help the children realise that a text can provide ideas, raise issues and facilitate discussion that goes beyond the confines of the page.

A sample lesson plan

Title and Genre of text:	Key Skill / Question Type: This highlights the specific skill to be taught and practised during each half term.
Warm up Questions: This part should be carried out first, with the purpose of orientating the children with the text and the genre provided.	**Essential Vocabulary:** These questions and activities support the Main Questions section. They increase children's knowledge and understanding of words and help promote an understanding of why certain words were chosen by the author.
Main Questions: This is the main body of the lesson and the types of questions posed here relate directly to the skill being practised. The same questions can be used for all three texts for each lesson and, where appropriate, the answers will be provided in brackets.	

Evaluative Questions:

This section does more than simply help the teacher to round off the lesson. It allows children to speculate on the tone and purpose of the text, as well as to consider the text's audience. It also enables teachers to ask further questions on the social relevance a text may have in today's society.

Planning Matrix*

This matrix gives an overview of how the various skills are developed throughout the series.

* Each ✓ = 1 half term lasting approximately 6 weeks.

Skill and Question type	Literal	Deductive	Inferential	Study Skills
Year 2	✓ ✓	✓ ✓	✓	✓
Year 3	✓ ✓	✓ ✓	✓	✓
Year 4	✓	✓ ✓	✓ ✓	✓
Year 5	✓	✓ ✓	✓ ✓	✓
Year 6	✓	✓ ✓	✓ ✓	✓

Overview of Year 5 lessons

Literal	Deductive	Inference	Study Skills
Going for Gold (A Reference Book)	Wolf Man (A Legend)	Hail Caesar! (A Speech)	What kind of Learner am I? (A Questionnaire)
Taekwondo (A Flyer)	Enjoy the Ride! (A Library Poster)	My English Rose (A Poem)	Genre (Library Classification)
Return to Planet Dread (A Blurb)	Colour Blind (A Metaphorical Poem)	Teddy's Bear (A Bedtime Story)	Pirates I (Using a Contents and Index Page)
Space Attack! (An Extract)	The Iron Man By Ted Hughes	Sweet Dreams (A Lullaby)	Pirates II (Using a Glossary)
Volcanoes (A Web Page)	Cragworth Cottage (An Advertisement)	Pieces of Eight (An Adaptation)	Anyone for T? (Using a Dictionary)
Birds of Prey (A Wildlife Chart)	The Tale of Two Cooking Pots (An African Tale)	The Magpie Girl (A Moral Dilemma)	Avalanche! (Using a Thesaurus)
	Txt Talk (Mobile Messages)	I Want My Mummy! (Instructions)	
	Hi Max! (A Handwritten Letter)	A Jockey's Life (A Fond Memory)	
	Murder at the Manor (A Murder Mystery)	The North Wind Doth Blow (A Fable)	
	Houdini Does it Again! (A Newspaper Report)	www.squashed tomato.com (A Film Review)	
	Tommy's Little Battle – Part I (A Narrated Poem)	The Quest II (A Film Script)	
	Tommy's Little Battle – Part II (A Narrated Poem)	Campfire's Burning! (Setting)	

Going for Gold

Non-fiction

Warm up Questions:

- Has anybody ever seen the Olympics? Did you enjoy them?

- Have you ever wondered how this huge sporting event first started? Today we are going to look at this very topic. What do you think its title might be?

- Write the real title on your wipe board. Why do you think the writer chose this title?

Main Questions:

1. Re-read paragraph 1. How do we know that the original Olympics took place? (because of artefacts we can see in museums) Draw your answer(s).

2. Re-read paragraph 2. Who banned the original Olympic Games? (Roman Emperor Theodosius I). Why did he do this if they were so popular? (he banned all non-Christian worship, and the Olympics were in honour of the Greek gods)

3. Re-read paragraph 3. Whose idea was it to bring the Olympics back to life? (Baron Pierre de Coubertin's)

4. Where and when were the first modern Olympics held? (Athens, 1896)

5. Fill in the table below:
   Who took part in the following Olympics?

	Ancient	First Modern	Today
Men			
Women			

6. What does this table show us? (today everyone has a chance to compete, not just the men)

7. Where and when was the Olympic flag first flown? (Antwerp, 1920) Describe to a partner what the different parts of the Olympic flag mean.

Essential Vocabulary:

- Highlight the word 'depicts'. Write it on your wipe board. Underneath, write the word 'picture'. Underline a spelling pattern you can see in both words. ('pict')

- What do you think the word 'depicts' means? (shows)

- Write the word 'competition' on to your wipe board. Now find the following words and tell a partner what you think these words mean: 'competing' (trying to be the best at something); 'competitor' (someone who takes part in a race or competition)

- What helped you work out their meanings? (they started with 'compete')

- Highlight the word 'ancient'. What is the difference between the words 'ancient' and 'old'? ('ancient' means historically very old, 'old' just means comparatively old)

- If something 'grinds to a halt', what do you think it does? (stops gradually, getting slower and slower) Show your teacher.

Evaluative Questions:

- Why do you think an illustration of a Greek boy was used rather than a Greek girl? (girls weren't allowed to take part in the ancient Olympics)

- Who do you think would enjoy reading this page the most, boys or girls? Why?

- Do you think male sportsmen get more fame and fortune than sportswomen? Why do you think this is? Do you think this is fair?

- Do you think the writer would agree or disagree with you? Why?

GOING FOR GOLD

So you want to know how the Olympics started, eh? Well, you would have to travel back almost 3000 years and well over 1000 miles to my home city of Athens to see that! Luckily, museums across the world house pottery that depicts men competing in the original games, in events such as running, wrestling and chariot racing. There are even records that date back to 776 BCE that list the names of past winners. Amazing or what?

I know what you're thinking. If the games were so popular, why did they disappear? That's an easy one - blame Roman Emperor Theodosius I! You see, the original games were held in honour of the Greek gods, so when he banned all non-Christian worship across the Roman Empire the games were forced to grind to a halt. It would take just over 1500 years and a Frenchman to breathe life into them once again.

It seems strange now, but when Baron Pierre de Coubertin, father of the modern Olympics, first dreamt of bringing back this ancient tradition, he found little support. However, after a lot of persuading, the first modern games took place right here in Athens! For ten glorious days in June 1896, around 245 men took part in 43 different sports such as discus and the long jump. Notice, though, I said 'men'. It would take another four years before women were allowed to compete (in golf, of all things) and another twelve before they were allowed on the track and field. How sexist!

And what about today? Well I'm sure you'll agree that the games seem to be going as strong as ever, with billions of viewers tuning in every four years to cheer on their favourite sporting heroes. Fantastic!

I'm off now. All this talk about the Olympics has inspired me to go out there and do some sport, so I'll leave you with a podium of Olympic facts I think you'll find interesting. Now, where did I leave my chariot…?

GOLD
In ancient times, competitors didn't receive medals but were awarded olive wreaths instead. Nowadays, a gold medal is given to the winner. Shhhh, don't tell anyone, but it is in fact 90% solid silver with 6 grams of gold laid on top.

SILVER
The five coloured rings were chosen because at least one of the colours appeared in the flag of each participating country. The five rings represent the five continents of the world and are linked together by sport.

BRONZE
The official Olympic flag was designed by Coubertin himself and was first flown in 1920 during the Antwerp games in Belgium, the first games to host a competitor from each continent.

Taekwondo

Non-fiction

Note to teacher – This lesson is best when you cut around the dotted lines and glue the two parts together. This will give your students a more authentic flyer for them to read.

Warm up Questions:

- Your teacher will show you some texts you might find posted through your letterbox. Can you guess what they might be? (Show them various texts: include a flyer)

- Today we are going to look at a flyer. Which text do you think is best described as a flyer? What do you think flyers try and do? (tell you about new activities or services)

Main Questions:

1. If you wanted to go to this club where would you go? Write the address on your wipe board. (Avondale Leisure Centre, Stockport SK3 0UP)

2. When would you go? (Monday 4pm & Friday 6:30pm)

3. What type of clothing should you wear? (any loose clothing)

4. When do you pay for your class? (when you go)

5. How much do you pay? (it doesn't say) Why do you think this important information is NOT on this flyer? (they might need to change the price, price may put people off)

6. Your brother Carl is 13 years old. Can he go with you, yes or no? (no) Which classes can he attend? (he would go with the adults Thursday 7pm, Sunday 6pm)

7. You want to ask if the classes are mixed. What should you do? (ring 0161 278 2080 or text 'TKD INFO' followed by your question to 07711529 354)

8. List three things the flyer suggests you will get better at if you go to these classes. (Body strength, fitness, flexibility, self-defence, more confident)

Essential Vocabulary:

- Which two words are written in capitals? Circle them. (ACTIVE, FREE)

- Why do you think the writer has done this? (they are important and will appeal to the reader)

- The prefix 'uni' = 1

- Look at the three types of bike. Draw the unicycle.

- Highlight the word 'unique'. What do you think this word means? (the only one)

- Highlight the phrase 'pop down'. Do you think this phrase is formal or informal? (informal, it means 'to come')

- When we use informal words and phrases we change the tone of a text. In pairs, look at the following words. Choose which ones best describe this text:

friendly	rude	welcoming	unfriendly
strict	warm	cold	relaxed

- Why do you think this? Make a list with your teacher.

Evaluative Questions:

- What do you think the main purpose of this text is? (a) to inform? (b) to persuade? (c) to entertain? (b) What is it trying to persuade you to do? (join the class and learn Taekwondo)

- Who do you think the target audience for this flyer is, children or parents? (parents) Why? (they are the ones who will pay for the classes)

- Where do you think you might see this flyer? (on your doormat, in libraries and schools)

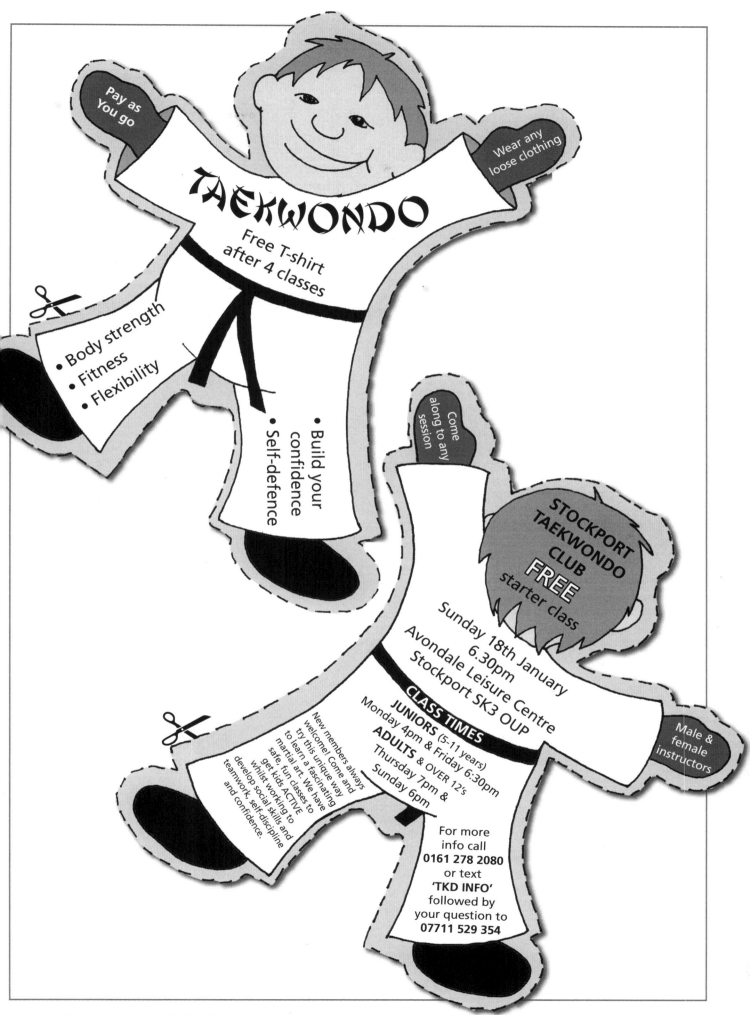

Return to Planet Dread

Non-fiction

Warm up Questions:

- Whereabouts on a book would you find the blurb?
  (a) front of the book?   (b) back of the book?
  (c) inside the book? (b)

- What sorts of things might you find in the blurb?
  Make a list with your teacher. Now look at the blurb for
  'Return to Planet Dread' and compare it to your list. Was
  there anything you needed to add to your list?

- What is the main purpose of this blurb?
  (to encourage people to read the book)

Main Questions:

Thinking about the book:

1. Who wrote 'Return to Planet Dread'? (Ian Podd)
   Who illustrated it? (L. Katowski)

2. How much does this cost in (a) Britain? (£5.99)
   (b) Australia? ($10.99)   (c) New Zealand ($12.99) Which
   company publishes this book? (Hopscotch Publications)

Thinking about the story:

3. Where is this story set? (deep in outer space)

4. Who is the likely hero in this story? (Captain Teller)

5. How many crew members begin this adventure? (ten)
   How many return? (one)

6. What do Captain Teller and his crew have to fight?
   (blood- sucking space zombies) Draw your answer.

Essential Vocabulary:

- Highlight the word 'quest'. Is a quest a long or a
  short journey? Is it one that is easy or difficult?
  (long and difficult)

- If the action is described as 'nail-biting' or 'keeps you
  on the edge of your seat' are you relaxed or tense?
  (tense) Show your teacher. Underline these phrases in
  the text.

- Do these two phrases imply that the story is exciting
  or boring? (exciting)

- Highlight the word 'gripping'. Grip hold of a pencil.
  Can you describe how you are holding it to a
  partner?

- When a book or film grips you, what does it
  grip, your eyes, your ears or your imagination?
  (imagination)

- What is *Return To Planet Dread's* ISBN number?
  (123 1 45678 123 4)

Evaluative Questions:

- As what genre do you think 'Return to Planet Dread' should be classified?

                  (d) science-fiction?

(a) romance?   (b) horror?   (c) comedy?   (d) science-fiction?

- Draw your answer. Why do you think this? Do you think this book is aimed at younger or older children?
  Why do you think this?

- Do you think this blurb is successful? How?

- Why do you think science fiction books are so popular if they are not real?

- What is this book's ISBN number? (123 1 45678 123 4)

RETURN TO PLANET DREAD

Ten blast off to save us. Only one will return.

"Computer, exactly how long have we got?"
Three minutes, twenty-four seconds and counting.
There was nothing more he could do. Captain Teller began running to his only hope...the escape pod!

Set in the not-too-distant future and far beyond the edges of known space, this latest chapter in the Star Quest series sees Captain Teller take on his most terrifying mission yet.

After a strange computer virus infects their ship, Titania, Teller and his crew are forced to crash land on the mysterious Planet Dread. All is not what it seems and ten soon become nine. With his ship down, his crew disappearing fast and no way of sending a message to Jupiter Station, Teller finds himself in a race against time and a fight against evil.

Join Teller and his crew as they battle to save Earth from blood-sucking space Zombies in Ian Podd's gripping new adventure 'Return to Planet Dread'.

Gold Medal

Winner of this year's Platinum Book Award.

"Nail-biting action from start to finish - a real page-turner. Britain's best selling author delivers again!"
The Evening Post

"A superb thriller that keeps you on the edge of your seat from page one. Podd at his best!"
Fan-Zone Magazine

Illustrated by L. Katowski
Hopscotch Publications

Price: UK - £5.99
Australia - $10.99
New Zealand - $12.99

ISBN 123-1-45678-123-4

1 231456 781239

Space Attack!

Narrative

Warm up Questions:

- Think back to the blurb for 'Return to Planet Dread'. Can you remember what this story was about? Where was it set? Who was its hero?

- Today we are going to read an excerpt from this book called 'Space Attack!' Do you think this will be set before or after Captain Teller crashes on Planet Dread? Why do you think this?

- Now read the text. Were you right?

Main Questions:

1. What is the name of Captain Teller's space ship? (Titania)

2. What is going to happen to this ship in five minutes time? (a) she will blow up and be destroyed? (b) she will be captured by blood sucking space zombies? (a) Draw your answer.

3. Where does the Captain tell his crew members to head for? (the planet)

4. Which crew member asks why Teller isn't coming with them? (Hayes)

5. When everyone except Teller has left, is the ship noisy or quiet? (noisy) What two things are making all the noise? (siren, steam) Draw your answers.

6. What colour are the flashing lights as Teller runs to his escape pod? (red) Why do you think this colour was chosen? (it's the colour for danger)

7. Why does Captain Teller not get into the escape pod? (he wants to save Titania)

Essential Vocabulary:

- Find a word that means 'a group of people who work on a ship or plane'. (crew)

- When Captain Teller orders the computer to 'stop' the countdown, which word does he use? (cancel)

- Highlight the word 'siren'. Do you associate this word with light or sound? (sound) Show your teacher how a siren might sound.

- Highlight the word 'bathing'. Copy this word on to your wipe board. Underline a word you can spot at its start. (bath)

- If you were 'bathing' in water, how much of your body would be wet? (all of it)

- What do you think the writer means when he says the ship was 'bathing' in red light? (it was totally immersed in red light)

Evaluative Questions:

- Do you think this part of the story is fast and exciting or slow and boring? (fast, exciting)

- The writer (Ian Podd) uses lots of ways to help him create such a story.

- Look at the checklist of dramatic conventions below:

Imminent danger	Nobody around to help you	A countdown to when the dangerous event will happen
Warning sounds	Warning or flashing lights	Lots of running around

- Can you find examples of how Podd uses these in his writing? How might reading such a fast and exciting story affect you as you read the story? How might it affect your own future writing style?

SPACE ATTACK!

Self-destruct in five minutes and counting.

'Will somebody turn off that stupid computer? Her voice is really starting to bug me'.

'I'm on it, Captain'.

'As for the rest of you, jump in the escape pods and head for the planet.'

'But Captain, aren't you coming with us?'

'Don't argue Hayes, that's an order. Now go. All of you!'

The surprise computer virus had been too much for Titania, Teller's oldest and most trusted friend, to bear. This flying rust bucket was the only place Teller called home and he sure wasn't going to let her fall into enemy hands. This was why he had set the self-destruct at five minutes. Long enough for his crew to escape. Not long enough to keep Titania in her misery a minute longer than she needed to be.

'Computer, exactly how long have we got?'

Three minutes, twenty-four seconds and counting.

There was nothing more he could do. Captain Teller began running to his only hope...the escape pod!

The self-destruct siren screamed down his ears, the flashing lights bathing everything in red. Steam hissed out of broken and battered pipes on every level.

Suddenly, he stopped. Not to catch his breath, but to give Titania a second chance.

'Of course! Why didn't I think of that before?'

Picking up a spanner he began racing towards engineering.

'Computer, this is Captain Teller, clearance code 2794, ordering you to cancel self-destruct.'

Clearance code confirmed. Self-destruct cancelled.

Perhaps today wasn't such a good day to die after all.

5

Volcanoes

Non-fiction

Warm up Questions:

- Draw a volcano erupting. Describe your picture to your group.

- What do you already know about volcanoes? Make a list with your teacher.

- If you wanted to find out more about volcanoes, in which type of book would you look? (a) a recipe book? (b) a reference book? (c) a dictionary? (d) a poetry book? (b)

Main Questions:

Look at the diagram.

1. When rock is very hot it melts. What do we call molten rock if it is below the Earth's crust? (magma) If it is above the Earth's crust? (lava)

2. As well as lava, what else do volcanoes 'spew out'? (poisonous gases, ash and cloud) Draw your answers.

Now look at the table.

3. In what year did Mount Etna erupt? (1669)

4. Which volcano killed 29,000 people? (Mont Peleé)

5. Where and when was the world's biggest volcanic eruption? (Tambora in Jambawa, Indonesia. 1815) How many people died in this terrible event? (92,000)

6. Which volcano killed more people, Mount Etna or Krakatau? By how many? (Krakatau 16,500)

7. Kelut appears twice on the list. Which eruption was the smallest 1586 or 1919? (1919)

Essential Vocabulary:

Read the poem.

- Circle the word 'anger'. How does the writer describe this word? (blazing)

- On a scale of 1 – 10, how hot is this word?

- If you were 'blazing with anger', how would you act? Show your teacher.

- With a partner, find three more words in the poem that mean 'very angry'. (rage, wrath, fury)

- Highlight the word 'unleashed'. Do you think this means (a) locked up? (b) tied up? (c) set free? (c) Why do you think this?

- Highlight the word 'devouring'. Do you think this means eating a little or a lot? (a lot) Why do you think this?

- Can you find the special name given to a scientist who studies volcanoes? (vulcanologist)

- If somebody were in a deep 'slumber', what would they be doing? (sleeping) Show your teacher.

Evaluative Questions:

- Which parts of this page confirm that this text is from a web page? (the labelled diagram, the table, the heading)

- Why do you think the writer has included the poem on this page? (to compare the volcano to a sleeping animal which wakes up angrily)

- In the conclusion, the writer continues his idea of a volcano being alive. How? (sleeping devils ... woken up from their slumber ... hell-bent on destroying)

- Do you think this is a good idea? Why? (it makes the volcano come alive like a living, breathing, evil monster - more memorable)

VOLCANOES

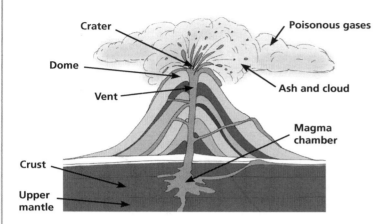

Crater
Dome
Vent
Crust
Upper mantle
Poisonous gases
Ash and cloud
Magma chamber

The beast begins to stir.
Suddenly he wakes!
His rage bursting forth,
With a mighty cry,
His blazing anger licks the sky.
Devouring everything in its path,
His wrath is unleashed,
His fury is unstoppable.

When a volcano erupts, we witness one of the most spectacular displays of nature's power known to man. Exactly when these beasts of beauty will wake, even vulcanologists do not know. But when they do, the cost can be great, not only to towns and farmland but also to human life.

Here is a list of the top ten most deadly volcanic eruptions to date:

NAME	PLACE	YEAR	NUMBER OF DEAD
Tambora	Jambawa, Indonesia	1815	92 000
Krakatau	Krakatau, Indonesia	1883	36 500
Mont Peleé	Martinique, West Indies	1902	29 000
Nevado del Ruiz	Armero, Colombia	1985	25 000
Mount Etna	Sicily, Italy	1669	20 000
Mount Vesuvius	Bay of Naples, Italy	79 CE	20 000
Kelut	Java, Indonesia	1586	10 000
Laki	Iceland	1783	9500
Santa Maria	Guatemala, Central America	1902	6000
Kelut	Java, Indonesia	1919	5000

And yet it would be unfair of us to simply view volcanoes as sleeping devils, waiting to be woken from their slumber and hell-bent on destroying everything before them. For when the beast falls back to sleep, and he will, then the ash and the lava that he has spewed forth will cool and harden and help shape the very Earth in which we live.

So just keep an eye on him for now. He is sound asleep, isn't he? And if he does begin to stir once more, then stand back in amazement and pray you're not standing in his way.

Birds of Prey

Non-fiction

Warm up Questions:

- Do you know what a bird of prey is? Which birds of prey do you already know? Make a list with your teacher.

Read paragraph 1.
- How many different kinds of birds of prey are there? (a) about 300?   (b) exactly 300?   (c) well over 300? (a)

- List three features that nearly all birds of prey share. (sharp talons, sharp eyesight, strong hooked beak) Draw and label each answer.

- The writer believes this makes them a very good hunting machine, true or false? (true)

Main Questions:

1. From how far away can a bird of prey spot a rabbit's ears twitch? (up to two miles)

2. Why aren't owls normally classified as birds of prey? (they like to swallow their prey whole)

3. Which bird of prey (a) hunts on the ground? (the secretary bird) (b) hunts from the sky? (the bald eagle) (c) doesn't like hunting at all? (the vulture)

4. Which of the three birds is usually bald? (a) the bald eagle? (b) the secretary bird? (c) the vulture? (c) Draw your answer.

5. With a partner, list two reasons for this. (it can stay cool and clean)

6. Why does the secretary bird not die from snakebites? (it has tough scales on its legs)

7. Which bird is a national symbol of America? (the bald eagle) Why do you think America chose this symbol? Make a list with your teacher. (colossal, powerful, strong)

Essential Vocabulary:

- Find a word in paragraph one that means 'as beautiful and as powerful as a king'. (majestic) Do you agree with this description? Why?

- Highlight the word 'plunge'. Is this a gentle or strong word? (strong) Is it fast or slow? (fast) Is it shallow or deep? (deep)

- Show your teacher how you would (a) plunge your hand into water; (b) plunge yourself into darkness.

- There is another fast word in this paragraph. Can you spot it? (snatching)

- Show your teacher how a person might 'snatch' a pencil from somebody.

- The writer uses a powerful adjective to describe the bald eagle's size. What is it? (colossal) What does it mean? (huge, enormous)

- Circle the word 'stun'. What do you think this word means? (knock out)

- Show your teacher how a person might look if they were stunned.

Evaluative Questions:

- Why do you think the writer calls these birds the 'kings of the sky'? (they are the biggest and most powerful birds)

- Do you think the writer enjoyed writing about these birds? Why do you think this?

- If you were to meet the writer of this page, what type of person do you think they would be? Why do you think this?

- What did you find most interesting on this page? Why?

- If you were writing this page, how would you improve it?

Birds of Prey

The kings of the sky, these majestic creatures have made the heavens their own. Although there are around 300 different species, nearly all share the same features needed to kill and butcher their prey. With dagger-like talons, razor sharp eyesight and powerful hooked beaks, they are living, breathing hunting machines. No wonder our fabulous feathered friends continue to fascinate us.

Talons	Eyes	Beaks
Normally the rear talon is the strongest and deadliest. Once this plunges into its victim's body, there is no escape. After snatching dinner from a lake or meadow, the talons grip hold of the feast while the bird flies to a nearby feeding post or back to its nest.	Piercing eyesight can scan for prey over a wide area. In fact, a special pit in the back of the eye gives them telescopic vision. This is so sensitive that they can spot the twitch of a rabbit's ears up to two miles away.	Hooked beaks act like sharp knives, tearing up the dead meat so that it is easier to eat. Interestingly, owls are not usually classified as birds of prey as they like to swallow their meal whole.

An American Beauty

The **bald eagle** truly is a colossal bird. Powerful and strong, its wingspan is wider than a man's height! Perhaps this is why the USA chose this magnificent bird as their national symbol. Like many fish eating birds, the bald eagle has bare legs so its 'socks' don't get wet during a fishing trip.

Snake Snack

With the longest legs of any bird of prey, the **secretary bird** attacks from the ground rather than the air. It uses its stilt-like legs to stun a snake by stamping on it. Tough scales on its legs protect it from any poisonous snakebite. It then deals the snake a deadly blow with its powerful back talon before grabbing it in its beak.

Scavengers

Members of the **vulture** family rarely hunt. They prefer to 'watch and wait' instead. The black vulture, for example, will simply circle a dying animal (or one that has already been killed) until it is safe enough to swoop down and pick the bones clean. This is probably the reason why some vultures look so ugly. The lack of feathers on their heads not only allows them to stay cool, but also keeps them clean... after all, it is easier to wipe blood off a bald head than off a set of beautiful feathers.

Wolf Man

Narrative

Deductive

Warm up Questions:

- What is a legend? (a traditional story)

- Which legend are we going to read about today? (the legend of a werewolf) What do you already know about this legend? Make a list with your teacher.

- Where is this story set? (Blackberry Hill) Who is the werewolf in this story? (Peter)

Main Questions:

1. Choose three words you think best describe the atmosphere of this story.

chilling	loving	friendly	tense	calm	nail biting

2. With your teacher, make a list of how the writer achieves this. Take turns in drawing your answers on a mind map where possible.

3. Was the storyteller related to Peter? (yes, Peter was his or her brother) What effect does this have on readers? (makes them more emotionally involved)

4. Was the storyteller scared as the werewolf was running towards him/her? How do you know? (yes – pounding heart, trembling hands)

5. Was the storyteller prepared for what might happen to Peter that night? How? (yes, by having a gun loaded with a silver bullet)

6. How many shots did the storyteller fire? (3) Were these loud or quiet? (loud – capital letters and exclamation marks)

7. When Peter died, was he a werewolf or a human? (human – his eyes had returned to blue) Do you think Peter enjoyed being a werewolf? (no – he thanked the storyteller for releasing him from this curse even though he was about to die)

Essential Vocabulary:

- Show your teacher how Peter 'dropped' to the floor.

- Was it slowly or quickly, lightly or heavily? (quickly and heavily)

- Circle the words 'growling' and 'snarling'.

- Show your teacher how these would sound.

- Why do you think the writer chose these two words? (they are animal sounds)

- Highlight the word 'trickle'.

- What do you think is trickling down the storyteller's face at the end of the story? (blood)

- Do you think there is a lot of blood or a little? (a little) Draw your answer.

- Highlight the word 'monstrous'. Is this a positive or negative word? (negative)

- Write down a word it reminds you of. (monster)

- What do you think the word 'monstrous' means? (to act like a monster)

Evaluative Questions:

- Why do you think this story is written in the first person? (because the events happened to the story teller)

- Did you think it made the story feel more or less real? How? (more real, because the writer describes exactly what happened and how they felt at the time)

- Who do you feel more sorry for, Peter or the storyteller? Why? (either the writer who had killed his or her brother, or Peter because he had been unhappy and now he was dead)

- Did you enjoy how the story ended? Why do you think it ended at this point? What do you think happens next?

Wolf Man

I had never stood on Blackberry Hill without the warm glow of a summer's sun before. But now, eerie shapes hung above me and an owl hooted somewhere in the darkness beyond. Trees swayed in the light breeze and the clouds drifted away to reveal a full circle of magic and madness.

Peter dropped to the floor. His eyes grew black and his back began to arch. His hair grew thicker and longer and before long he had grown both claws and fangs.

For a while he did nothing. Silence. Then, without warning, he stood on his two back legs and gave out a bloodcurdling howl. And at that very moment I knew that it was not Peter who now stood on Blackberry Hill but a werewolf – half man, half wolf!

The legend was true.

As I watched from behind a bramble bush, this monstrous creature began to sniff the late November air. Suddenly, he stared straight into my eyes and began running towards me.

My heart began to pound. My hands began to tremble. There was only one thing that would stop him now - a silver bullet. I pulled out my gun and waited. Closer and closer he came, growling and snarling as he ran. And when he jumped in the air to pounce on me....

BANG! BANG! BANG!

Slowly the werewolf changed back to Peter. He turned his head. 'Thank you,' he whispered and closed his blue eyes. The monster was dead but so was my brother - shot through the heart.

The village was safe once again.

As I walked home I felt something wet and warm trickle down my cheek. I touched my face and looked at my red fingers in the moonlight. In the fight Peter had scratched me.

Was the curse of the werewolf really over?

Only time and the next full moon would tell...

Enjoy the Ride!

Non-fiction

Warm up Questions:

Your teacher will show you the first line of this text.

■ What do you think the writer is asking us to do? (go on a journey) How is this supported by the title? ('Enjoy the Ride!' suggests a journey) Underline the word(s) that make you think this.

■ Why do you think the writer starts with the word 'dare'? (the journey might be scary but it will also be an adventure)

Main Questions:

Look at the poem on the back of the book.

1. Does the poet think boys, girls or boys and girls should read more? (boys and girls)

2. Draw the face of one of the children who is reading in the poem.

3. How do we know that (a) they are enjoying reading? ('smiles on their faces, eyes open wide') (b) they are interested and excited about what they are reading? (reading is compared to a fantastic journey)

4. Who do you think might be their 'trustworthy guide'? (their teachers, parents or older siblings)

5. Does the writer think words are sometimes hard to understand, yes or no? (yes)

6. Highlight the word 'journey'. Is this a long or short trip? (long) What is the writer trying to tell us when he uses this word? (that reading is a journey which will last all your life)

7. Do you think the writer thinks that learning to read is worth the effort? (yes) Why? (if you can read, there is so much that you can learn and enjoy)

Essential Vocabulary:

■ Can you find a word that means 'to want to know more' in the 3rd question? ('curious')

■ What do you think to be 'whisked away' means? Find it in your text. (to be taken away quickly)

■ Which ride does the writer use to describe our emotions? (roller coaster) Draw your answer.

■ Why do you think the writer describes our emotions in this way? (because they rush up and down)

■ Highlight the word 'fantastical'. Do you think this is a real word? (no) Why? (it's a made-up word which describes new worlds). Choose from the list below two words you think were used to create it: terrific, fantastic, cool, magical, brilliant, great.

■ Highlight the word 'plunge'. When you plunge into a swimming pool, what do you think you are doing? (jumping quickly into a completely different environment)

■ Why do you think the writer uses this word? (in the same way as going into water, you are completely submerged in the story)

Evaluative Questions:

■ Do you think the writer of this poster enjoys reading? (yes) Why do you think this? (they are enthusiastic)

■ Where do you think you would see this poster? (at a library entrance, in a book shop)

■ What do you think the overall aim of the poster is? (to encourage reading)

■ Who do you think the poster is aimed at? (children) Why do you think this?

■ Do you think the poster is successful? Why?

Enjoy the Ride!

Dare you jump on board the Reading Express?

Are you brave enough to experience the thrills
and spills of action and adventure?

Are you curious enough to be whisked
away to explore fantastical strange new worlds?

Will your heart be strong enough to ride the
emotional roller coaster of a love story or
plunge into the terrifying darkness of a mystery?

So what are you waiting for?

Long, long ago in a faraway land,
Sat a boy and a girl with a book in their hands.
With smiles on their faces and eyes open wide,
They travelled along with their trustworthy guide.
And as they adventured over hill and through page,
The words came alive as though freed from their cage.
So journey they did with a feeling so grand,
For the book they were reading,
They could now understand.

Once upon a time...

Don't just stand there, watching everyone else have all the fun. Pick up a book today and set off on the greatest journey of your life!

If you haven't got your ticket yet, just ask at Reception. And what's more, it's free!

TICKET

Colour Blind

Poetry

Deductive

Warm up Questions:

- Copy the title of the poem onto your wipe board. What do you think this poem will be about?

Read paragraph 1.
- Who is blind? (Deborah) Has she always been blind? (Yes)

- What question does the poet ask her? ('Do you dream your dreams in colour, black or white?')

- Why do you think the poet asks her this question? What do you think her answer will be?

Main Questions:

Read paragraph 2.
1. Despite being blind, is Deborah a happy person? (yes smiles)

2. Does Deborah dream in colour, black or white? How do you know? (colour, 'rainbow pots and spotty dots')

Read paragraph 3.
3. Is the poet polite to Deborah?
   (Yes- 'if you would be so kind')

Read paragraph 6.
4. Your teacher will show you each colour that Deborah describes. Find it in the poem and highlight it.

5. Does Deborah see each colour as positive (+) or negative (-)?

Read the last two lines.
6. Draw the poet's eyes when these lines are spoken. Are they open or closed? (closed)

7. What, then, do you think the final line means: to physically see, to understand or to experience? (to understand)

Essential Vocabulary:

- Highlight the word 'tender'.

- Is this a warm or cold word? (warm)

- Is it hard or soft, with love or without love? (soft, with love)

- What two words does Deborah use to describe her school shirt? ('crisp, clean')

- What does this tell us about (a) the shirt itself? (washed and freshly ironed) (b) Deborah's mother or father? (they look after her well)

- Show your teacher how Deborah found the poet's eyes to close them.

- Was it fast or slow, gentle or rough? (slow and gentle)

- Why do you think the poet describes her fingers as if they are walking? (they move across the eyelids like two feet)

- What does this tell us about Deborah? (she uses her touch to find out about things and to communicate)

Evaluative Questions:

- Do you think Deborah allows her disability to stop her experiencing life? (no)

- Your teacher will now give each of you an object. Close your eyes.

- Touch it, smell it, listen to it. What colour do you do you think it is? Why?

- Has this poem helped you to understand visually impaired people better? How?

Colour Blind

I met a girl called Deborah,
She'd been born without her sight.
I asked her 'Do you dream your dreams in colour, black or white?'

She paused and smiled and turned to me,
With laughter in her eyes,
'In rainbow pots and polka dots,' she said, to my surprise.

'Then explain to me,' I said to her, 'if you would be so kind'
'How touch and taste and smells and sound paint pictures in your mind'.

Her hands reached out, her fingers gently walked across my face.

And when she came upon my eyes,
As tender as a rose,
She whispered softly,
'Listen to the words I speak'.
And my eyes she then did close.

Red is a fiery temper, a slamming door, a blazing row.
Blue is the taste of salty tears and long goodbyes, of waves crashing on lonely rocks.
Yellow is the warm kiss of a summer's glow, the golden taste of honey.
Green is the smell of freshly cut grass, brown of autumn leaves.
Grey is the sitting on a cold concrete floor; it is the colour of boredom.
And white? Well white is the putting on of a crisp, clean shirt on a Monday morning.

She paused for thought… My thoughts.

'Now do you see?'

'Yes. I see clearer now than I have ever done before'.

The Iron Man
by Ted Hughes
Narrative

Warm up Questions:

■ What do you already know about the writer of this story? (he was more famous for being a poet than a children's author)

Read the first three paragraphs.
■ Where is the Iron Man standing? (at the top of a cliff)

■ Is this scene set during the day or at night? (at night) How do you know? ('in the darkness')

■ What do you think will happen next? Read on to see if you are right.

Main Questions:

1. Is the Iron Man big, and if so, how big? Make a list with your teacher. ('taller than a house', 'head .. as big as a bedroom', 'eyes like headlamps')

2. On a scale of 1 – 10, how strong do you think the wind was that night? Give a reason for your answer. ('he swayed in the strong wind that pressed against his back')

3. Do you think the Iron Man would be heavy? (yes) Why do you think this? (iron is heavy and the Iron Man is huge)

4. How does this affect his movement, is it fast or slow? (slow)

5. When the Iron Man falls, is it quiet or noisy? (noisy) With your teacher, make a list of words that suggest this. ('CRASH! bumping, clanging') Circle them in your text.

6. When the Iron Man breaks up, was it into many pieces or only one or two? (many) How do you know? (different parts fell off, 'all the separate pieces', 'lay scattered far and wide')

7. Was the sea calm that night, yes or no? (no) What makes you think this? ('the sea went on boiling and booming')

Essential Vocabulary:

■ Find the word 'brink'. Put a box around it.

■ Do you think this word means the Iron Man was:
   (a)   standing quite close to the edge of the cliff?
   (b)   standing on the very edge of the cliff?
   (c)   far away from the edge of the cliff? (b)
   Draw your answer.

■ Find a phrase that shows us how the sea acted on the edge of the rocky beach. ('chewing away at the edge of the rocky beach') Show your teacher how this would look and sound.

■ Why do you think Ted Hughes uses this idea? (it is as if the sea is hungry and eating away at the beach)

■ Copy the word 'CRRRAAAASSSSSH!' onto your wipe board.

■ Count the number of each letter in this word. (1 C, 3 Rs, 4 As, 5 Ss, 1 H) What do you notice? (increase in number of letters as if the word is growing in volume)

■ Do you think this is a spelling mistake or that he has done this on purpose? (on purpose)

■ Why do you think he repeats the word 'CRASH' three times shortly afterwards? (it makes you think of the waves beating against the rocks again and again)

Evaluative Questions:

■ Does the fact that this is how Ted Hughes starts 'The Iron Man' surprise you? (yes) Why? (you wonder how his story can be told now he has gone)

■ How do you think Ted Hughes' work as a poet has influenced his writing? (he is using words carefully to make the reader imagine the scene; parts of the text read like poetry)

■ Can you spot pieces of the text that sound more poetical or where, like a poet, he plays with the structure or punctuation of the text? Make a list with your teacher. Highlight them on your sheet.

The Coming of the Iron Man –
original version from '*The Iron Man*'
by Ted Hughes.

The Iron Man came to the top of the cliff.

How far had he walked? Nobody knows. Where had he come from? Nobody knows. How was he made? Nobody knows.

Taller than a house, the Iron Man stood at the top of the cliff, on the very brink, in the darkness.

The wind sang through his iron fingers. His great iron head, shaped like a dustbin but as big as a bedroom, slowly turned to the right, slowly turned to the left. His iron ears turned, this way, that way. He was hearing the sea. His eyes, like headlamps, glowed white, then red, then infra-red, searching the sea. Never before had the Iron Man seen the sea.

He swayed in the strong wind that pressed against his back. He swayed forward, on the brink of the high cliff.

And his right foot, his enormous iron right foot, lifted – up, out, into space, and the Iron Man stepped forward, off the cliff, into nothingness.

CRRRAAAASSSSSH!

Down the cliff the Iron Man came toppling, head over heels.

CRASH!
CRASH!
CRASH!

From rock to rock, snag to snag, tumbling slowly. And as he crashed and crashed and crashed

His iron legs fell off.

His iron arms broke off, and the hands broke off the arms.

His great iron ears fell off and his eyes fell out.

His great iron head fell off.

All the separate pieces tumbled, scattered, crashing, bumping, clanging, down on to the rocky beach far below.

A few rocks tumbled with him.
Then
Silence.

Only the sound of the sea, chewing away at the edge of the rocky beach, where the bits and pieces of the Iron Man lay scattered far and wide, silent and unmoving.

Only one of the iron hands, lying beside an old, sand-logged washed-up seaman's boot, waved its fingers for a minute, like a crab on its back. Then it lay still.

While the stars went on wheeling through the sky and the wind went on tugging at the grass on the cliff-top and the sea went on boiling and booming.

Nobody knew the Iron Man had fallen.

Night passed.

3

Cragworth Cottage

Non-fiction

Warm up Questions:

- Highlight the initials 'B & B'. What do you think they stand for? (bed and breakfast) What is the name of this B & B? (Cragworth Cottage)

- In what part of Britain is it? (the lowlands of Scotland) Who runs it? (Mr and Mrs McKenzie)

- Name two things you can do while you stay at Cragworth Cottage. (relax, go fishing, climbing, biking, canoeing, visit a castle)

Main Questions:

1. What standard is this B & B? (a) very high? (b) average? (c) very poor? (a) How do you know? (4 thistles) What does this suggest to you? (a high standard)

2. Is the castle near or far away from the cottage? (near – 'a stone's throw away') Can the same be said of the fishing? (quite near – 10 minutes' drive)

3. Do you think the fire in the cottage is gas, electric or wood burning? (wood burning – log fire) Do you think this fire gives out a lot of heat or a little? (a lot - roaring)

4. Answer true or false: babies can stay at the cottage (true); dogs can stay at the cottage (true)

5. In pairs, look at the list below and draw which you think Cragworth Cottage is probably surrounded by: hills, shops, rivers, trees, lakes, busy streets, rocks, factories. Why do you think this? Does the rest of your group agree with you?

6. If you wanted to 'see' the inside of Cragworth Cottage, would you (a) drive up to Scotland and ask the McKenzies if you can look inside? (b) telephone the McKenzies and ask them to e-mail you some photographs? (c) visit their website? (c)

Essential Vocabulary:

- Circle the word 'perched'. Draw a bird perched on a branch.

- Now perch your pencil on the edge of a table. What do you think it means? (balanced on the edge)

- How near is Rob's outdoor centre to the lake? (very close) Draw your answer.

- Highlight the words that describe the breakfast. ('hearty' and 'home cooked')

- Do you think these words are positive or negative words? (positive) Why?

- Which of these words tells us that the breakfast is big and filling? (hearty)

- Would you describe the term 'home cooked' as (a) warm or cold? (b) friendly or unfriendly? (c) inviting or uninviting? (warm, friendly and inviting)

- Can you find any other examples of warm, friendly and inviting words? Make a list with your teacher.

Evaluative Questions:

- Where are you likely to see this text? (in a tourist information or holiday brochure) What do you think the main aim of this text is? (a) to tempt the reader to book a room? (b) to tell the reader how great Scotland is? (a)

- Why do you think this text begins with (a) a quote and (b) 4 thistles? (to encourage the reader to look at the rest of the ad, to validate its quality)

- What type of holidaymaker do you think would enjoy Cragworth Cottage the most? (someone who enjoys the outdoor life and also a comfortable place to stay) Why? (Cragworth Cottage would provide everything they wanted)

Cragworth Cottage

'Highly Recommended'   Best of British B & B Guide

Welcome to Cragworth Cottage, where we open our front door with a warm heart and an even warmer smile.

Wipe your feet on our welcome mat and join us in the Lowlands of Scotland –
a place that really does have something for everyone:

 • Dramatic landscapes on your doorstep

 • The historic Stirling Castle just a stone's throw away

 • Trout fishing less than 10 minutes' drive away

 • Or for the more adventurous: mountain biking, rock climbing and canoeing – all available at Rob's Outdoor Sports Centre, perched on the edge of Loch Lomond.

And what do you do when you return from your day's excitement? Well, simply take off your coat, put up your feet and relax next to a roaring log fire. And after taking in a good night's sleep, wake up to a hearty home-cooked breakfast. What could be better?

To ensure you have a relaxing stay, our two main bedrooms both have king-sized beds and en suite facilities. The third has bunk beds with a separate bathroom downstairs. Cots are available on request.

And don't forget, your four-legged friends are also welcome.

Situated just two miles from the beautiful village of Aberfoyle, Cragworth Cottage gives you the peace and quiet you deserve and the rest and relaxation you need.

So why not let your hosts, Mr and Mrs McKenzie, look after you while you discover what makes Scotland the place to be this winter?

For a detailed price list and a virtual tour of your home from home, come and visit us at
www.cragworthcottage.co.uk or telephone us directly on **01786 475019.**

The Tale of Two Cooking Pots

Narrative

Deductive

Warm up Questions:

- What does the word 'tale' in the title of the text suggest to you? (this is a story)

Read paragraph 1.
- Who is the main character of this tale? (Kisimba) Where is she going? What do you think she is going to do when she gets there? (she is going to the river to fetch some water)

- Does this opening paragraph suggest this tale will be set in Britain? Why? (no, the Molopo river is in Africa)

Main Questions:

1. The Tale of Two Cooking Pots is from Africa. Highlight evidence to prove this on your sheet. (Kalahari Desert, Molopo River)

2. Is Kisimba rich or poor? How do you know? (poor because she has to go a long way to fetch water and she lives in a tin shack)

3. When Kisimba sets off to the river, is it light or dark? How do you know? (dark – 'before the sun started to rise') Why do you think she sets off so early? (it will be cool then and she has a long way to go)

4. On a scale of 1 – 10, how strong do you think Kisimba is? Why do you think this? (8 – 'as strong as an ox', but she is old)

5. Can you think of an adjective to describe Kisimba's character? (hard-working, determined, kind, resourceful) Write it on your wipe board. Now show it to your group and say why you have chosen this word. Do they agree or disagree with you? Why?

6. Is the cracked pot upset by what the perfect pot says? How do you know? (yes, because a last drop of water runs down, like a tear)

Essential Vocabulary:

- Underline the word 'frail'. Pretend to be somebody who is frail. Show your teacher. What does this word mean? (weak, delicate)

- Highlight the word 'barren'. Do you think this is a positive or negative word? Why? (negative because nothing grows)

- Find the word 'perfect' and circle it. What do you think the opposite of this word will be? Write it on your wipe board.
  unperfect   disperfect   imperfect (imperfect)

- Add the 'im' prefix to the following words. What do you think they mean?
  possible   polite   patient   personal

- Are these positive or negative words? (negative; they mean the opposite of the original words)

- Can you find an 'im' word in this tale that means 'not perfect'? (imperfection)

- Circle the words 'splashes' and 'speckling' in the penultimate paragraph. Does the writer use these words to show:
  (a) the colourful flowers cover all the earth?
  (b) the colourful flowers cover the earth here and there? (b). Draw your answer.

Evaluative Questions:

- How might a person be 'cracked' or 'imperfect'? (if they are disabled in any way, none of us is perfect)

- What do you think the moral of this tale is? (that even if we think people are imperfect, they can still be valuable)

- What does this tale teach us about how we should view disabled people? (we should look for what they can do, rather than what they can't do)

- Do you think this moral applies only to African people? Why? (no, it applies to people all over the world in different situations)

- How can this moral apply to British people? Can you think of a real example?

THE TALE OF TWO COOKING POTS

Each day, before the sun began to rise and the birds began their morning chorus, Kisimba would begin her long journey down to the banks of the Molopo River.

Although the years had made her look frail and helpless, Kisimba was, in fact, as strong as an ox and as wise as a kilio bird. She thought nothing of travelling the great distance for her daily water - life in the Kalahari had made her that way.

Over her shoulders, on each end of a long wooden pole, she would carry two cooking pots; and while at the river fill them both to their brims. And as dawn began to break she would return to the tin shack she called home.

Yet despite all this hard work, when she finally arrived at her doorstep she had only one and a half pots of water for her effort. Why? Because one of the two cooking pots was cracked and was unable to contain all the water that it had been given.

"Just look at the state of you," moaned the perfect pot. "You're leaking everywhere! Perhaps we should replace you with a pot that can fulfil its duties".

The cracked pot sighed and one last drop of water ran down its side and dripped onto the dry African soil.

"Perhaps he is right. Perhaps you should replace me with a better pot".

Kisimba's smile glowed as she gently stroked the pot. Her words were warm and kind, like the butterflies that were beginning to visit the morning's garden.

"Why do you think the air smells so sweet and the birds and the bees and the butterflies all sing and dance around us? I'll tell you why. I always knew you were a leaky cooking pot, so down one side of the lane I planted many flowers. And as we passed, your imperfection gave way to a most wonderful picture. Look...."

And as the old cooking pot turned around he saw before him splashes of colour speckling the red earth that surrounded them.

"It was you who helped me to bring colour and life, laughter and love into such a barren land. Why would I replace you when you bring me so much joy?"

Txt Talk

Poetry

Warm up Questions:

- Why do people send texts? Make a list with your teacher.

- What do you notice about how the title 'Txt Talk' is spelt? (it is spelt as if it were a text) Is this a mistake? (no) Why not? (it reflects what the lesson is about)

- Imagine you wanted to send the following message. How might you text it? *Sebastian, can you meet me before six o'clock? Thanks mate.*

- Why do you think people text like this? (to save space and time)

Main Questions:

1. Draw a picture of what you might wear to Phil's party. Explain your choice. Why might Phil want to know if you are coming to the BBQ before Wednesday? (so that he can get the right amount of food)

2. Which text is from somebody who is ill? (the fourth one, from J) Why do you think this person wants her mum to text rather than phone her? (she has a sore throat and can't speak) What do you think the 'J' stands for at the end of this text? (a name)

3. What do you think the relationship between 'J' and her mum is like? (trusting, caring, close) Why do you think this? (J is asking her mum for help, knows that she will help, ends with love and kisses)

4. Which phone will not be able to text much longer? (the third one) Why? (it is nearly out of credit)

5. Which text does NOT use informal text talk? Why do you think this is? (the fifth one because it is from a cinema and not between friends)

6. Did the sender of the bear joke find it funny? (yes) Explain why you think this joke made him laugh. (he put LOL which means 'laugh out loud', played with the word 'pause')

Essential Vocabulary:

- Is text talk formal or informal? (informal)

- On a scale of 1–10, how informal do you think text talk is?

- Highlight the following text talk on your sheet and fill in the table below:

Informal	Formal
B4	
L8	
Cud	
wen	
2	
Sat	
Soz	
Luv	
Pls	

- Can you spot any more of your own? Add them to your table.

- Read the following message. Write it down formally on your wipe board.
  Phn me wen u get in 2nite. I wana spk 2 ure mum. Thanx.

  {Phone me when you get in tonight. I want to speak to your mum. Thanks}.

- Do you think using these abbreviations is a good thing? Explain. (it's good because it saves time and money)

- Why do you think texting in this way might be a bad thing? (encourages bad spelling habits)

Evaluative Questions:

- Look at each text.

- Why do you think it has been written? Give reasons for your answers.

  To request   To invite   To apologise   To inform   To entertain

- As a group, do you think mobile phones are a good or bad thing for children to have? Make a 'for' and 'against' list with your teacher.

Txt Talk

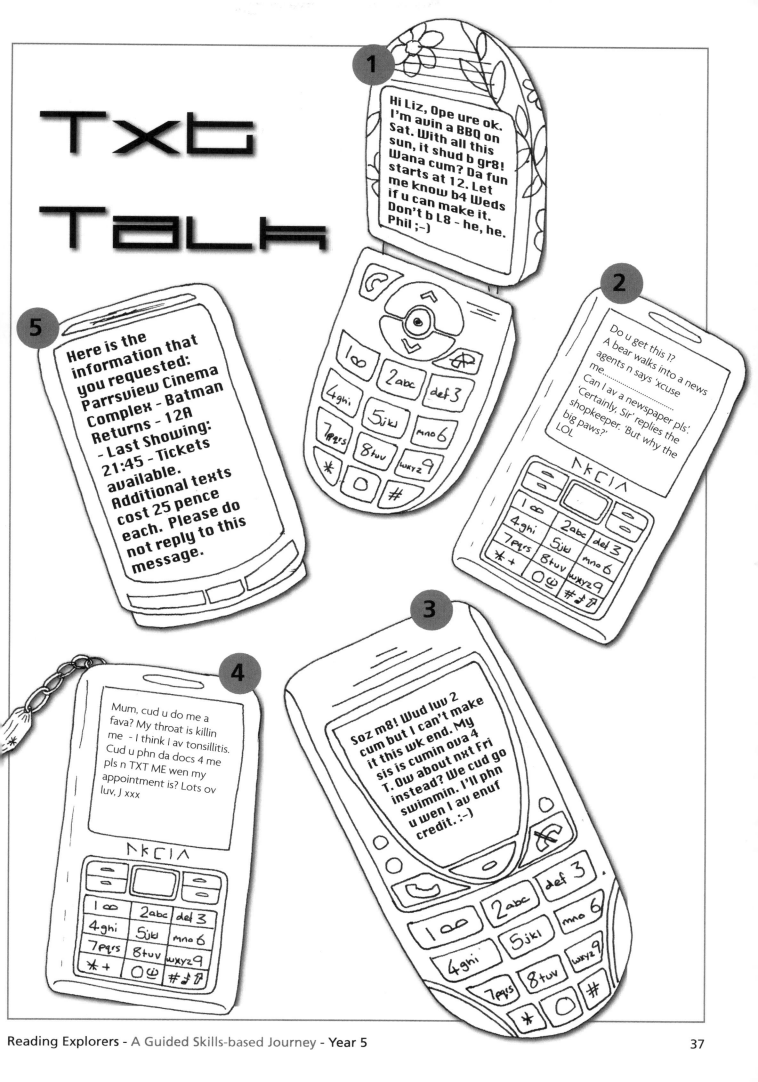

1. Hi Liz, Ope ure ok. I'm avin a BBQ on Sat. With all this sun, it shud b gr8! Wana cum? Da fun starts at 12. Let me know b4 Weds if u can make it. Don't b L8 - he, he. Phil ;-)

2. Do u get this 1? A bear walks into a news agents n says 'xcuse me.................. Can I av a newspaper pls.' 'Certainly, Sir' replies the shopkeeper. 'But why the big paws?' LOL

3. Soz m8! Wud luv 2 cum but I can't make it this wk end. My sis is cumin ova 4 T. Ow about nxt Fri instead? We cud go swimmin. I'll phn u wen I av enuf credit. :-)

4. Mum, cud u do me a fava? My throat is killin me - I think I av tonsillitis. Cud u phn da docs 4 me pls n TXT ME wen my appointment is? Lots ov luv, J xxx

5. Here is the information that you requested: Parrsview Cinema Complex - Batman Returns - 12A - Last Showing: 21:45 - Tickets available. Additional texts cost 25 pence each. Please do not reply to this message.

Hi Max!

Non-fiction

Warm up Questions:

- Look at how this letter starts. Does this suggest the letter will be formal or informal? (informal) How? ('Hi!' is informal - formal letters start with 'Dear')

- Who wrote this letter? (Leigh) Do you think the writer of this letter will be young or old? Why? (young – goes to school)

Main Questions:

1. Why can't Leigh ride the bike? (a) because it's raining? (b) because it's broken? (b) Draw your answer:

2. What do you think Max has done to himself?
   (a) bruised his leg?   (b) cut his leg? (c) broken his leg? (c) Draw your answer.

3. When do you think this happened?
   (a) during half term? (b) during the Christmas holidays? (c) during the summer break? (c)
   Why do you think this? (The letter is dated 23rd September)

4. If Max visits Leigh, how will he travel? (a) by coach? (b) by plane? (c) by train? (d) by taxi? (c) Draw your answer.

5. Which city is Leigh most likely to be from? (a) Manchester? (b) Cardiff? (c) Liverpool? (d) Birmingham? (e) London? (c)
   Why? (Watching Chelsea v Liverpool - Come on the Reds!)

6. After reading the whole letter, why do you think Leigh's family has moved house? (the family needed more room due to the baby)

7. Read the 'P.S.' at the end of Leigh's letter. Why do you think Leigh has written this letter by hand? (they are not yet connected to the internet)

Essential Vocabulary:

- There are lots of names in Leigh's letter. Names can be formal or informal. Can you find: (a) two examples of formal names (Mr Turnbull, Mrs. Watkins) (b) two examples of informal names (Pat, Chris, Max, Sam)

- Many of the informal names Leigh uses can be used for boys or girls.
  Circle the following names on your sheet and fill in the table below:

Name: (short form)	Masculine	Feminine
Chris	Christopher	Christine
Pat	Patrick	Patricia
Max	Maxwell	Maxine
Sam	Samuel	Samantha

- Do you think the writer of this letter (Leigh) is a boy or a girl? Why do you think this?

- 'Leigh likes technology'. Is this statement true or false? (true – doesn't like old-fashioned ways)

- Highlight some technological words and phrases that suggest this. (interactive, computer, download, internet)

- There are two words that are stressed in paragraph six. How and why are they stressed?
  (WARNING – capitals to show danger.
  Still – underlining emphasises the length of time)

Evaluative Questions:

- Why do you think Leigh says 'sorry' at the start of her letter? (harder to read, thinks Max might see it as old-fashioned too)

- Why do you think Leigh's mum disagrees with her? (perhaps she doesn't use e-mail, hand written letters warmer, heart-felt, more personal)

- Is the tone of the letter important when you are writing a letter? (yes) How? (it can sound friendly or unfriendly, formal or informal). If Leigh had sent this letter electronically, do you think its tone would be different? (yes) How? (typing looks more formal and less personal and you can't add drawings)

- Who do you agree with: Leigh, mum or both? Why?

23rd September

Hi Max!

Sorry for writing to you the old-fashioned way but I can't e-mail at the moment. Mum says that the old-fashioned ways are best but I don't think I agree with her. Anyway, it's raining cats and dogs outside so I've got plenty of time on my hands just as well really seeing as my bike's got a puncture. It's not stopping Barkley from digging up the garden though. Trust Chris to give him a bone!

How are you? Hope you're feeling better after your fall. It won't be long before the plaster comes off and you're skating again. Have many people signed it by the way?

I know it's only been a few weeks but I'm enjoying my new class and have started to make some good friends. Mr Turnbull isn't half as funny as Mrs Watkins though. We went on a school trip last week to visit a museum called 'Body Zone'. It was much more interesting than I thought it would be. Lots of the exhibits were interactive. I learnt loads! Did you know that over 90% of our body is made up of water? I wonder why we don't freeze solid during winter then?

Our new house is great. I've got my own room at last. As the eldest I also got to choose the biggest bedroom. I can even lock Pat out when I'm on the computer. Ah, peace at last!

Dad says you can come down in half term and stop over (but only if you promise to leave your skateboard at home). Let me know whether or not you can make it. Mum says that we can pick you up from the station no problem and that the rail fare is pretty cheap.

WARNING: Little Sam is <u>still</u> crying through the night keeping us all awake. And so is the smell of dirty nappies. Bring some ear plugs and a peg!

I'm off to watch the footy now. Chelsea are playing Liverpool. Come on the Reds!

See you soon eh?

Leigh

P.S. Thanks for the gift voucher. I'm thinking of downloading some music off the internet once we're connected.

Murder at the Manor

Narrative

Warm up Questions:

- Look at the title. What type of text do you think this will be? (a detective story) Why? (murders usually are mysteries which have to be solved)

- Imagine you are a detective. Answer the following questions to get the key facts of this case.

- Where has this crime taken place? (in the study at Hawthorn Manor)

- Who has been murdered? (Lord Toffsbury)

- In which room has the murder been committed? (in the study)

- Who discovered the body? (Lady Toffsbury)

Main Questions:

1. What season is it, spring, summer, autumn or winter? (winter - snow)

2. What type of party do you think the Toffsburys were having that night? (a) a barbeque? (b) a Halloween party? (c) a bonfire night party? (d) a Christmas party? (d) (Lady Toffsbury was wearing a sparkly dress)

3. Is Lady Toffsbury cold? (yes, she asks for a blanket) Why do you think this is? (the window is open and it's a winter's night)

4. What time do you think this crime took place? a) 10.30 am? (b) 3.00 pm?   (c) 7.00pm ? (d) midnight? (c) What clues make you think this? (guests were arriving)

5. How do you think the killer escaped? (through the window) Why do you think this? (the door was locked from the inside)

Essential Vocabulary:

- Highlight the word 'ruffled'. Is this hard or soft? (soft) Show your teacher. Ruffle a friend's hair.

- What were the crows doing before the scream? (roosting - sleeping)

- Do you think it was a man or a woman who screamed and disturbed them? (a woman) Why do you think this? (sharp scream of a woman)

- What sound did the crows make? (cawed) Show your teacher.

- The writer likens this sound to 'an old hag'. Why? (it sounds like cackling)

- Draw a picture of an 'old hag' on your wipe board.

- A group of crows is called 'A Murder'. Circle the word 'murderous'. What do you notice? (it has 'murder' in it)

- Why do you think the writer describes the crows 'like a murderous storm cloud'? (it adds to the eerie atmosphere, they are black and form a cloud shape when they fly)

- How did the Inspector walk into the study? (briskly) Is this a fast walk or a slow walk? (fast) Show your teacher. Walk 'briskly' to your desk.

Evaluative Questions:

- The text is broken up into two parts. Why? (the first part is setting the scene; the second part is the action)

- Do you think it was a good idea to include both the fox and crows at the start of the story? Why? (a good idea – it adds to the scary atmosphere)

- Who do you think might have killed Lord Toffsbury? Why might they have done this?

Murder at the Manor

The moon looked down as a silver fox thieved its way across the snow covered grounds of Hawthorn Manor and hid in the shadows of Timperley Wood. A slight wind ruffled the feathers of the crows that were now roosting high in the trees.

Only the sharp scream of a woman broke the silence – the crows cawing like an old hag as they flew into the sky like a murderous storm cloud.

Soon afterwards, a phone call was made to the village police station.

'Inspector Doyle to see you, Ma'am.'

'Thank you Sasha, do show him in. Oh, and could you bring me a blanket, please? It's awfully cold in here'.

Inspector Doyle took off his gloves; placed one in each pocket of his trench coat and walked briskly into the study. There, slumped over his writing desk, was the body of Charles Toffsbury, Lord of the Manor and husband of Lady Josephine Toffsbury, who now sat in a large leather chair on the other side of the room. Her emerald coloured ball gown glistened in the moonlight.

'Oh Inspector, it's simply too dreadful to speak of. He was fine an hour ago. I was speaking to him myself. Then, when he didn't join me to greet our guests, I came in here to look for him.' Josephine Toffsbury buried her head in her hands.

'Has anybody touched the…er…body, your Ladyship?'

She shook her head. 'No, they couldn't have. The door was locked from the inside and only my husband and I have a key. Oh, and Sasha of course, but that goes without saying.'

'And who would this Sasha be, your Ladyship?'

'That would be me, Inspector. I'm the head butler here at Hawthorn Manor'.

As he spoke he wrapped a blanket round Lady Toffsbury's shoulders and walked over to the window. He was just about to close it when…

'If you don't mind, Sir' said the Inspector politely, 'I'd rather nothing in the room was touched, including the window. This is, after all, a crime scene.'

Houdini Does it Again!

Non-fiction

Deductive

Warm up Questions:

- What kind of report is this? (newspaper report) How do you know? Make a list with your teacher.

- Name the following:
  The newspaper (Daily Herald)
  The journalist (Chuck Washington)
  The photographer (Montgomery Smith)

- Who is this report about? (Houdini) What did he do? (dived into the freezing River Hudson while he was handcuffed). Where did this event take place? (Hudson River, New York)

Main Questions:

1. Do you think this newspaper is British or American? (American) Draw the flag of the country for your answer. How do you know this? (it costs 10 cents)

2. In which season did this event happen, spring, summer, autumn or winter? (winter). There are two clues that tell us this. What are they? (December 14th, ice on river)

3. Was the atmosphere exciting or boring? (exciting) Highlight the phrase that tells you this. (The atmosphere was electric)

4. When Houdini escaped, was the crowd happy? (yes – they clapped and cheered). Was the clapping loud or quiet? (loud). Write down the word that tells us this. (thunderous) What do you think this word means? (noisy like thunder) Why? (it has the word 'thunder' in it)

5. Was this Houdini's first ever escape, yes or no? (no) Circle the word in the headline that tells you this. (Again!)

6. Do you think this event was organized, yes or no? (yes) How do you know? (there were divers to make sure Houdini was safe)

7. Do you think Harry Houdini is still alive today? Explain why you think this. (No, because this happened nearly 100 years ago)

Essential Vocabulary:

- Highlight the word 'escapologist' and write it on your wipe board. Underline a word root you can spot at the start of this word. (escape)

- What kind of tricks do you think 'escapologists' do? (they get out of dangerous situations)

- As the crowd watched, did time appear to pass quickly or slowly? (slowly)

- There is a word that tells you this. Highlight it. (limped)

- How would you walk if you had a limp? Show your teacher – limp to your desk.

- Find a word in the final paragraph that means 'to amaze'. (dazzle)

Evaluative Questions:

- Do you think Chuck Washington enjoyed reporting this event? Why? (yes, in the last paragraph he hopes that Houdini will dazzle audiences for many years to come) How would you have felt if you had been watching?

- Do you think the newspaper should have included a safety notice telling their readers not to try and copy Houdini's stunts? Why?

- If Houdini was alive today, what would you like to ask him and why? If you wanted to find out more about Harry Houdini, what could you do?

Daily Herald

December 14th 1912   10 cents

Houdini
Does it Again!

A report by Chuck Washington

Photograph by Montgomery Smith

Drama in the Hudson River

Young and old alike were treated to a spectacle like no other yesterday when Harry Houdini, world famous escapologist, completed one of his most daring stunts yet.

The crowd of New Yorkers looked on as the Hungarian-born showman climbed a nearby bridge and raised his handcuffed wrists. After carefully studying a small hole in the ice, he then dived into the freezing waters of the Hudson River and was gone. This was theatre at its best!

One and all held their breath as the minutes ticked by: one… three… five… seven… The atmosphere was electric.

After eight long minutes had limped by, trained divers began to climb down a rope in order to give a helping hand to their missing magician. But there was no need. No sooner had they reached half way, up popped Houdini, greeted by wild cheers and thunderous applause.

When asked how he had managed to escape such a trick, he simply replied: "A true magician never reveals his secrets. But remember, I did once work as a locksmith". And with nothing more than a wink and a smile, he was whisked away, presumably to warm up.

How long Houdini can hold onto his secrets is not known. However, this reporter, for one, hopes that they can remain locked away for some time so that he can continue to dazzle his audiences, both here and abroad, for many years to come.

Tommy's Little Battle, Part I

Poetry

Warm up Questions:

Read the title of this poem.

- What do you think the main character will be like? (young) Why? (Tommy can be a child's name and his battle is little)

- What do you think a 'little battle' might be? (overcoming a fear)

- This poem is narrated. What job does a narrator do? (tells a story)

- How many verses does this narrated poem have? (eight)

- Underline the words that rhyme that show this is a poem rather than a story.

Main Questions:

1. Do you think we will read the complete poem today? (no, it is only 'part 1')

2. Where is Tommy during this poem, the kitchen, the bathroom or his bedroom? (in his bedroom) How do you know? (he heard the tap downstairs and leapt out of bed)

3. When Tommy woke up, did he do so quickly or slowly? (slowly) Which line in verse 2 tells us this? ('Tommy's eyes yawned open')

4. What does Tommy do in verse 5 that suggests he is scared? (he hides under the covers) Show your teacher.

5. Do you think Tommy likes sport? Draw two things that suggest this. (cricket bat and baseball cap)

6. In which verse does the poet change Tommy's name to 'Tom'? (verse 7) What does this tell us about Tommy's character? (that he's being grown up and is changing his personality, that he is growing up by deciding to face his fear)

Essential Vocabulary:

- Read line 1 out loud. Did you read it quickly or slowly? (slowly) Why? (dripping is slow)

- What helped you make this decision? (the punctuation slows the words down)

- Why do you think this idea is repeated in verse 6? (it reminds the reader of the problem that hasn't gone away)
Look at the three faces below.

- Which do you think is Tommy, which is Tom and which is Thomas? (Tommy is the child, Tom the old man, Thomas the posh man) Why? (those forms of the name go with each type of face)

- Highlight the word 'commence' in the final verse. Do you think it means 'to start' or 'to end'? (to start)

Evaluative Questions:

- Who do you think the Nark really is, a monster, ghost or Tommy's cat? (Tommy's cat) Draw your answer. In pairs, list three reasons why you think this.

- What does this tell us about Tommy? (that he has a strong imagination)

- Why do you think the poet chose to end part one where he did? (to make the reader want to find out what happens next, he's about to go into battle).

- What do you think will happen next? (Tommy will go downstairs to confront his fears)

Tommy's Little Battle

Part I

Drip, drip, drip,
Dripped the tap downstairs.
Beating like a tin drum,
Waking up nightmares.

Tommy's eyes yawned open,
And he peered into the dark.
'What's going on?' he thought at once.
A monster, ghost or Nark?

Now a Nark's a type of gremlin,
With a cutlass and a hat.
He lives there in the kitchen,
Riding Samson, Tommy's cat.

He laps the milk and murders mice,
He's fierce and hard to catch.
And in the deepness of that night,
Tommy heard his sharp claws scratch.

His covers tight around him
Tommy's bed became his cave.
He might be scared, but knew full well,
That darkness, safety gave.

Drip, drip, drip,
The Nark he never died.
And Tommy knew right there, right then,
There was no place to hide.

He took a breath, leapt out of bed,
And grabbed his cricket bat.
The Nark just roared with laughter.
Tom now wore his baseball hat.

So Tom was dressed for battle,
And the fight could now commence.
Braver than a lion,
He could jump the highest fence.

Tommy's Little Battle, Part II

Poetry

Warm up Questions:

- What was the title of last week's text? (Tommy's Little Battle, Part I) What type of text was it? (a poem)

- Who was its main character? (Tommy) Why did he change his name towards the end of this poem? (he became braver)

- With a partner, put the following sentences in the correct chronological order:
  1. The noises from downstairs activate Tommy's imagination
  2. He decides to confront his fears and investigate
  3. Tommy is awoken by a dripping tap
  4. He grows scared and tries to hide (3, 1, 4, 2)

Main Questions:

1. What time is this scene set? (midnight) How do you know? (it was dark and the clock struck twelve) What effect does this have on (a) the reader (makes the reader know that it is scary) (b) Tom? (makes Tom determined to confront his fears)

2. Read lines 1 and 2. How do we know Tom is still scared? (his heart beats quickly as he tiptoes downstairs)

3. How do we know in the next two lines that Tom has an active imagination? (the darkness made him think of grizzly bears)

4. When Tom enters the kitchen, is he confused? (yes) What does he do to suggest this? (he scratches his head) Why do you think he is confused? (there is nothing there)

5. How do you think the Nark escaped? (through the cat flap) What does this tell us about the Nark's size? (it's not very big)

6. Did the Nark leave the kitchen a long time ago or quite recently? (recently) How do you know? (the cat flap is still flapping)

7. Re-read the final verse. What lesson does (a) Tom and (b) the reader learn? (both learn that you must confront your fears)

Essential Vocabulary:

- Which words tell us that verses 3 and 4 are noisy? (smashing, made such a din, kafuffle, crashed) Make a list with your teacher.

- On a scale of 1 – 5, how noisy would you rate these words?

- Which of these words is a nonsense word? Write it on your wipe board. (kafuffle)

- What do you think it means?

- Highlight the word 'destroy'. Is this a strong word or a weak word? (strong)

- Which of the words listed below comes from the same spelling root?

destiny	destruction	design
destroyer	desperate	destructive

(destruction, destroyer, destructive)

- Write them on your wipe board.

- What helped you make this decision? (they all begin with 'destr' and they all mean something to do with destroying)

Evaluative Questions:

- Who do you think this poem is aimed at? (a) younger children? (b) older children? (c) teenagers? or (d) adults? (b)

- Why do you think this? (the main character is a similar age and deals with a problem they will be familiar with – scared of the dark)

- What do you think Tom is really fighting, the Nark or his imagination? (his imagination)

- Why do you think this poem has been written? (to encourage people to confront their fears)

Tommy's Little Battle

Part II

Yet still his heart beat quickly,
As he tiptoed down the stairs.
The shadows there beneath him,
Made him think of grizzly bears.

The clock now sang her chorus,
Twelve times she cried with joy.
Her hands now clapped, her face now looked,
On Tom and not the boy.

And as he turned the handle,
Of that heavy kitchen door.
Out came a great kafuffle,
And a smashing on the floor.

Tom knew the Nark was angry,
Having served up such a din.
Bottles smashed, pots, pans did crash,
Yet still Tom entered in.

But as he did, the cat flap flapped.
The Nark had simply fled.
'What's that noise?' a voice cried out.
Tom stood and scratched his head.

'Nothing much, I dropped some milk.'
Tom thought of what he'd done.
He knew he'd won the battle,
But the war was far from won.

For as in life, from time to time,
The dripping tap returned.
But never would old Tom forget,
What that six year old had learned:

As nightmares come and go through life,
The Narks you must destroy.
Stand tall, my friend, and conquer all,
Then life you will enjoy.

Hail Caesar!

Non-Fiction

Inferential

Warm up Questions:

- What do you already know about the Roman Empire? Make a list with your teacher.

- Did the Romans conquer parts of Britain? (yes)

- How many items does this Roman soldier have to collect altogether? (13) Which two items has he yet to collect? (cooking pot, thick cloak) Draw your answers.

Main Questions:

1. Who do you think Caesar was, a foot soldier, an army officer or the Emperor? (the emperor) Why do you think this? ('Hail Caesar!' is a form of praise)

2. Who do you think gave the speech at the start of the text, a foot soldier, an army officer or Caesar himself? (an army officer) Why do you think this? (he is speaking directly to the soldier)

3. Write down the question the officer asks the soldier. (Are you ready for the battle ahead?) Do you think the soldier replied by shaking or nodding his head? (nodding) Show your teacher. Why do you think this? (next word after question is 'good')

4. Were the soldiers well armed? (yes, 2 javelins, a dagger and a sword) Were they prepared for all weathers? (yes, wool for sandals, woollen cloak and tunic) Were they well fed? (yes, enough grain for 15 days) Were their camps well protected? (yes, they had stakes)

5. Why do you think the Roman Empire was so successful? (the army was well-equipped and well-organised)

Essential Vocabulary:

- Highlight the word 'Hail'. Do you think this is a strong or weak word? (strong) What do you think it means, 'hello' or 'praise'? (praise) Why? (it is said about the emperor, not to him)

- What does the officer call the soldier? (Soldier) Why do you think he does this? (he doesn't know his name)

- What words are used to describe items made from the following materials? wood (wooden); metal (metallic); wool (woollen)

- Copy them onto your wipe board. What do you notice? (they all have suffixes which mean 'made of' added on to the original word)

- Highlight the two words 'victory' and 'defeat'. How does the officer describe these words? (sweet taste, bitter poison) Why do you think he does this? (those will be the sensations of victory or defeat)

Evaluative Questions:

- Put a box around the part of this page that should be spoken, not written. (the first part, down to 'Hail Caesar!')

- Your teacher will now play the role of the Roman officer. As your teacher speaks, follow the words on the page and underline the words that are stressed. Compare the words you underlined with the rest of your group.

- Why do you think these words were stressed and not others? (they are important)

- With a partner, take it in turns to be the army officer giving this speech to his soldiers. Act it out! Your teacher will watch you.

- Imagine you are the soldier in the picture. What effect would this speech have on you? Why?

HAIL CAESAR!

Soldier - Prepare yourself for the battle ahead, for we are at war with anyone who is an enemy of the Roman Empire! Be strong and you will drink down the sweet taste of victory. Be weak and you will taste the bitter poison of defeat! Brother, a hero's welcome awaits you back home, but only if you do not die like a dog.

So then soldier, are you ready for battle and glory? Good, then the battle is already won and victory is ours for the taking!

Hail Caesar!

A ROMAN SOLDIER'S CHECKLIST:

1. A leather or metal helmet. ✓
2. Body armour – a bronze or iron breastplate with leather straps, worn over a woollen tunic. ✓
3. Leather sandals – stuffed with wool in winter. ✓
4. A thick woollen cloak – also for winter.
5. Wooden shield – soaked in water before a battle so it won't burn. ✓
6. 2 javelins (with metallic tips) to hurl at your enemy. ✓
7. Small sharp dagger – kept in a leather scabbard with a wooden or bone grip. ✓
8. A longer double-edged sword – again, a scabbard is needed to keep this weapon safe. ✓
9. 15 days' supply of grain to eat. ✓
10. Cooking pot.
11. 2 stakes - for building a fence around your camp. ✓
12. Pick or shovel to dig with. ✓
13. A double-headed axe. ✓

My English Rose

Poetry

Warm up Questions:

- What do you think about when you see a rose?

- When do people give roses and why?

- A red rose is also the national flower for which country: England, Ireland, Scotland or Wales? (England)

- Now look at the title of this poem. What do you think the poem will be about? Why?

Main Questions:

1. Do you think the 'Rose' in this poem is (a) a flower? (b) a person? (b)

2. Why do you think the poet gave the main character this name? (a beautiful rose eventually withers and dies)

3. Re-read verse 5. Draw a picture of what is happening in this verse. Do you think this verse is important? (yes) Why? (it marks the change from positive to negative)

4. How did people see Rose when she was younger? (beautiful) Why? (she was young and fresh)

5. How do people see Rose now she is old? (grey, worn out)

6. Highlight the word 'withering'. Write it on your wipe board. Underline the root word 'wither'. When and why might a plant 'wither'? (when it has flowered for a long time and its energy has gone) Why do you think the poet has used this word to describe Rose's touch? (it is no longer soft and gentle)

7. Re-read the lower part of the poem. How else does the poet infer that Rose is an old person who is forgotten? (dim light in the fog, sun setting, black and white photograph, dusty album)

Essential Vocabulary:

- Do you think 'Rose' is a boy's name or a girl's name? (girl's) Why do you think her parents gave her this name? (it reminded them of a beautiful flower and they loved her very much)

- Look at the following girl's names: What time of year do you think they were born?

Holly	Daisy	Robin	Lily
winter	summer	winter	summer

- Why do you think this? (we associate those names with the different seasons)

- Highlight the word 'stir'. Show your teacher how you might stir a cup of tea. If something stirs inside you is it fast or slow, strong or gentle? (slow and gentle)

- There are two words in verse 6 that mean the opposite to 'bright'. (faded, dim) Can you spot them?

Evaluative Questions:

- Who do you think would understand this poem best?
  (a) a school pupil? (b) your teacher? (c) an old person? Why do you think this?

- Do you think the tone of this poem is happy or sad? Why do you think the poet chose this tone?

- After reading this poem, do you view old people differently? How might this affect how we treat old people when we see them?

My English Rose

Yesterday her beauty shone as brightly as the sun's rays
and brought happiness into the hearts of all who gazed upon her.

Yesterday her sweet perfume would kiss the sky
and stir a warm glow in those who held her close.

Yesterday her touch was soft, gentle
and her tenderness would comfort the broken-hearted.

Yesterday she was wanted, loved.

But time pushes forward like a sailing boat on the
waters of life.

Today her beauty has faded to grey
a dim light in the fog of old age.

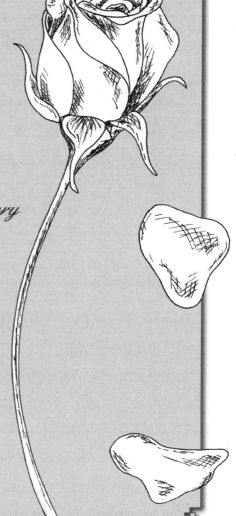

Today her sweet perfume is floating away on a memory
a setting sun on a winter's day.

Today her soft, gentle touch is withering
a black and white photograph in a dusty album.

The love that once blossomed is no more.

Teddy's Bear
Non-fiction

Warm up Questions:

Read the first line.
- What type of text do you think we will be reading today, factual or fiction? Why do you think this?

- Who do you think the audience for this text might be? (young children) Why do you think this? (it begins 'Are you sitting comfortably?')

Main Questions:

1. After reading the whole text, who do you think it was written for? Y2   Y3   Y4   Y5   Y6 (Y2)
   Why do you think this? Make a list with your teacher.

2. What does Teddy Roosevelt do to show us he cannot shoot the bear? (put down his gun and turned his back)

3. What does this tell us about his character? (he was kind)

4. Clifford Berryman called his cartoon 'Drawing the Line in Mississippi'. What do you think this phrase means? (deciding to do what is right)

5. The writer ends this story with the word 'happily…ever… after'. Why? (because slowing down points to the end of a story)

6. Do you think he would have said these words quickly or slowly, loudly or quietly? (slowly and quietly)

7. If you were reading this text to a child in Year 2, how might you read it? (slowly and quietly) Think about your tone of voice, volume and pace. Practise with a partner and show your teacher.

8. Why did you choose to read aloud like this?

Essential Vocabulary:

- Highlight the word 'beckoned'. Your teacher will now beckon to you. What do you think this word means? (ask someone to come towards you without speaking) Now 'beckon' another member of the group to sit next to you.

- Circle the two words 'tired' and 'exhausted'. Draw a line to link them. Which word is stronger? (exhausted) How would you look different if you looked 'tired' and then 'exhausted'? Show your teacher.

- Find the word 'cartoonist'. What do you think this person's job is? (drawing cartoons in a newspaper or magazine) Why do you think this?

- How does the writer describe the black bear? (fluffy) Why do you think he chooses this word and not 'hairy'? (fluffy sounds more cute)

- Look at how Teddy Roosevelt said 'Yes!' to Morris Mitchtom's idea. Does this show us that (a) he liked the idea? (b) he loved the idea? (c) he was unsure about the idea? (b) What makes you think this? (he was enthusiastic)

Evaluative Questions:

- Do you think this story is true or not? Why?

- Why do you think the writer chose to write this factual piece in a storybook style?

- Did you enjoy this style of writing or did you find it too babyish? Discuss. When might you want to write in such a style?

- Re-read the first and last line of this text. Why do you think the writer included these lines if they were not part of the story?

Teddy's Bear

Are you sitting comfortably? Then close your eyes and I'll begin...

Once upon a time in a land far, far away, there lived a strong and powerful ruler. His name was Theodore Roosevelt (his friends called him 'Teddy' for short) and he was the 26th President of the United States of America.

One cold November, he was out hunting in a place called Mississippi. All day long he looked and he looked for a bear he could shoot but, alas, he could not find one.

He was just about to give up when one of his men beckoned to him to come closer. There, in front of him, was a little baby bear, tired and exhausted and very, very frightened.

So sad was this sight that the president could not bring himself to shoot. He put down his gun and turned his back on the fluffy black bear.

News of this story soon spread and the very next morning people all over America woke up to read about it over breakfast.

A cartoonist named Clifford Berryman even drew a picture to go with the story. He called it 'Drawing the Line in Mississippi'.

A hop, skip and a jump away, in a city called New York, sat a shopkeeper, Morris Mitchtom. When he read the story he liked it very much and asked his wife to make two small bears to put in his shop window.

Everybody fell in love with the two small bears and Morris asked the president if he could call them after him? Teddy said 'Yes!'

And so the teddy bear was born and little boys and little girls everywhere could sleep happily... ever... after.

The End.

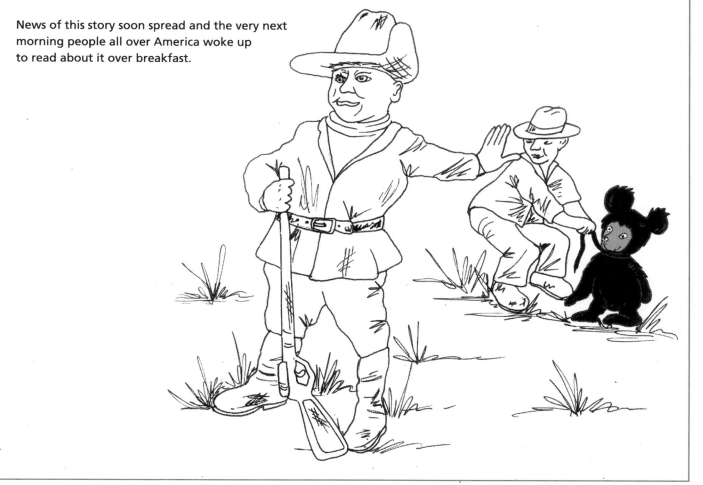

Sweet Dreams

Poetry

Warm up Questions:

- Write down the title of this text. (Sweet Dreams) What does it suggest this piece of writing might be about? (going to sleep)

- If you were to read this title out loud, how might you say it? (softly) Show your teacher.

- Why did you say it in this way?

Main Questions:

1. When is a lullaby more likely to be sung, in the morning, the afternoon or the evening? (in the evening)

2. How would you sing a lullaby? Choose from the list below:

quickly	gently	slowly	aggressively
softly	loudly	forcefully	sweetly

(softly, gently, slowly, sweetly)

3. If you wanted to play a guitar while singing, would it be electric or acoustic? (acoustic) Why? (softer sound)

4. Which other musical instruments might you play with a lullaby? (clarinet, harp, piano) Draw your answer and discuss why you have chosen this with your group.

5. When do you think he might have written this lullaby? (a) when his children were babies? (b) when his children began going to school? (c) when his children had grown up? (a)

6. Why do you think he called his lullaby 'Golden Slumbers'? ('Golden' = precious, valuable and 'Slumbers' = deep sleep)

7. Who do you think would have the sweetest dreams, the parent or the baby? (the baby) Why? (the lullaby was sung to the baby)

Essential Vocabulary:

- How does the writer picture a baby's cry? Draw your answer.

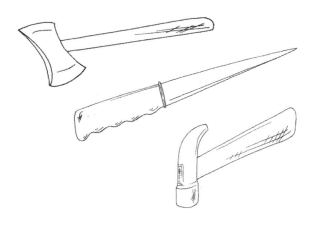

- Do you think this is a positive or negative image? (negative)

- Circle another negative word the writer uses in this paragraph. (sharp)
  How does this word contrast with the title? (it has the opposite meaning)

- Find two words in paragraph 4 that describe a place a baby might sleep. (cradle, crib)

- Highlight the word 'gonna'. Is this word meant to be spoken or written? (spoken) Is it formal or informal? (informal) If you were to write this word formally, how would you do it? (going to)

- Why do you think the words in these lines are repeated in the first and last paragraphs? (it's like the chorus in a song)

Evaluative Questions:

- Why do you think lullabies have survived so long? (they're handed down from one generation to the next)

- Do you think the writer of this page is a man or a woman? Why?

- Who do you think this page is written for, men, women or both?

- Do you think the writer has any children of his or her own?

- What do you think is most important in a lullaby, the tune or the words? Why?

Sweet Dreams

Hush little baby don't you cry,
Mama's gonna sing you a lullaby.

When a new babe is born, it is a time for much rejoicing - and rightly so. But if your baby does not sleep soundly and your nights are always being interrupted, then this joy can soon turn into a nightmare. A baby's cry is sharp enough to slice through even the deepest of sleeps.

So how can we help our little ones drift off to Never Never Land and stay there till the break of dawn?

One trick parents like to use is to sing a lullaby. These soothing songs are often passed down through families by parents and grandparents. The lullaby below is a lovely example of this. Written by the English poet Thomas Dekker, it has provided peace and quiet in houses up and down the land for over three hundred years.

In Old English, these beautiful tunes were called 'Cradle Songs' and were sung as parents gently rocked their baby's crib.

Usually a lullaby promises a reward for good behaviour, and though the baby is too young to understand the words being sung, their soft melody and soothing tones help create an atmosphere that is relaxed and peaceful, two important ingredients for the perfect night's sleep.

So hush little baby don't you cry,
Mama's gonna sing you a lullaby.

Pieces of Eight

Narrative

Warm up Questions:

- Looking at the title, what genre of text do you think this might be? (a novel about pirates) Why? (pirates' parrots say 'pieces of eight')

- Looking at the text itself, does this confirm your initial ideas? (yes) How? (the action takes place on a ship and the men are murderers)

- This text has been adapted from the classic children's book 'Treasure Island', written by Robert Louis Stevenson in 1883. Why do you think somebody might do this? Make a list with your teacher.

Main Questions:

1. Treasure Island was written in first person by its main character Jim Hawkins. Can you find three words that prove this? (me, myself, I) Why do you think R. L. Stevenson wrote Treasure Island in this style? (it reads like a diary)

2. Where on the ship is he? (down in the bottom of the ship)

3. Do you think this scene is set in the day or at night, is it quiet or noisy? (at night, quiet) Make a list with your teacher of things that suggest this. (darkness, sleep, rocking the boat gently, the boat was singing) What effect does this have on you as the reader?

4. In paragraph eight, why do you think the modern writer likens the crew to bears waking from hibernation? (they are big and fierce, their sleep was deep so they woke slowly)

5. Show your teacher how the words 'pieces of eight' might be spoken. Why do you think these words are repeated over and over again? (sharp, loud like an alarm clock)

6. How many words does Long John Silver speak? (four) What might this tell us about his character? (he was strong - used to giving orders and being obeyed)

Essential Vocabulary:

- Highlight the word 'bairns'. Do you think this is a modern word or old-fashioned? (old-fashioned) Why do you think the modern writer has used such a word? (to show that the story took place a long time ago)

- What do you think 'bairns' are? (children)

- Circle the word 'petrified'. On a scale of 1 – 10, how scared do you think Jim was? (10) Why? (he was going to be discovered, he could not move)

- Highlight the word 'chuckling'. Is this type of laughter big or small, loud or quiet? (small and quiet) Why do you think R. L. Stevenson used this word? (to show Jim couldn't laugh noisily for fear of waking them up)

- Now find the word 'shrill'. Why do you think R. L. Stevenson used this word to describe Captain Flint's cry? (it shows a contrast to all the quietness. It was high pitched and ear-piercing)

- Underline the word 'shudder'. Show your teacher how you might shudder in your sleep. What does this suggest you are doing at the time? (dreaming)

Evaluative Questions:

- Do you think it is right for a difficult story to be adapted for younger readers? (yes, it makes it easier for them to read the story) What do you think R. L. Stevenson would think if he knew? (he would be pleased to think he had some new readers)

- Do you think it is important that the modern writer kept Stevenson's characters, events and style of writing the same? (yes) Why? (it is like the original, but simplified)

- Do you like the fact that Jim is telling us the story, not an adult? Why?

- What do you think happens to Jim after Silver and his men discover him?

Adapted from Treasure Island by Robert Louis Stevenson (1883)

Pieces of Eight

Darkness cloaked me as I walked deep in the belly of the ship, and not one of the men who were with me stirred from their sleep. If it were not for the occasional snore or a restless shudder, I would not have known they were there at all.

The boat, rocked gently by the watery hands that held her, seemed to be singing to her bairns, the creaking lullaby of a true Pirate Queen.

I remember chuckling to myself and thinking how funny it would be if I lay down beside the men and joined them in their dreams. How their faces would look as they awoke to find me in their midst, a boy amongst murderers and thieves.

Then, all of a sudden, a shrill voice broke forth out of the darkness.

'Pieces of eight... Pieces of eight. Pieces of eight... Pieces of eight'.

Captain Flint! Silver's green parrot had given me away.

My heart pressed heavily against my chest and I dared not breathe in case I did let out a scream.

The dark shapes that surrounded me began to stir from their slumber like shadowy bears awakening from their winter's hibernation. And yet so petrified was I that I myself was frozen to the very timbers I was standing upon.

'Who goes?' came the voice of Silver.

I dared not answer.

'A light!' cried the voice of Silver once more. And as the footsteps and the voices of the crew grew ever louder, I knew I was doomed to be discovered.

The Magpie Girl

Narrative

Inferential

Warm up Questions:

- Which bird is the main character of this story associated with? (magpie)

- What is this bird well known for? (attracted to bright, shiny objects) How might this knowledge inform you about the girl's character? (she liked bright, shiny things too)

Main Questions:

1. How does the writer describe the apples? (they shone like rubies) Why? (the juicy apples look precious in the girl's eyes)

2. Underline the line the magpie girl speaks. (It's only one apple. It's only one apple.) Do you think she says these words out loud or in her head? (in her head) Why do you think she repeats this sentence? (she is trying to convince herself that stealing one apple isn't so bad)

3. Do you think the woman buying the apples is rich or poor? (rich)

4. Why do you think the writer includes this character? (to emphasise the difference between her and the magpie girl)

5. There are seven apples in the story. Who owns them? (the lady had six, the magpie girl had one) Why do you think the writer gave the seventh apple to the magpie girl? (the seventh magpie in the poem had a secret, as was her stealing)

6. How do we know how she feels about stealing? (she knew that the apple would not taste as sweet as the stallholder had promised)

7. Why does the magpie girl think a stolen apple will taste differently from one bought? (she will feel guilty eating it)

Essential Vocabulary:

- What word does the writer use to describe the magpie girl's eyes? (heavy) Does this suggest she is tired or wide-awake, happy or sad? (tired and sad)

- Which words does the writer use to describe how her dreams disappeared? (floated away) Does this suggest they disappeared quickly or slowly? (slowly)

- Highlight the word 'blur'. Write it on your wipe board and blur it. Why do you think the writer likens this word to fog? (it becomes indistinct like things do in fog)

- Which words are written in italics? (only one) Why do you think they are written in this way? (to stress repitition)

- Circle the word 'nudged'. Show your teacher how you might 'nudge' someone.

- Do you think the woman was nudged by accident or on purpose?

- Highlight the word 'bustled'. What do you think this word means? (was busy, crowded)

Evaluative Questions:

- Was it right for the magpie girl to steal the apple?

- Why do you think the writer included the poem at the start of this story?

- Why do you think the writer set this scene on a cold, wet December evening?

- Highlight the most important line in this part of the story. (the final sentence) What do you think the writer is trying to say? Do you agree or disagree? Why?

The Magpie Girl

One for sorrow, two for joy,
Three for a girl and four for a boy.
Five for silver, six for gold,
Seven for a secret never to be told.

Her heavy eyes fixed themselves on the apples across the cobbled street, as they shone like rubies in the setting December sun.

The cold air nipped at her fingers and bit at her toes and her frosted breath drifted away in much the same way her dreams had done many moons before.

'Come on ladies. Get your apples. Get your juicy apples'.

The winter rain made her hair cling to her face and her rags cling to her body.

'Come on now, tuppence ha'penny for four. A bargain I tell you'.

The cries of the stallholder started to blur, as though a fog was wrapping itself around his words. And all she could think about was that for the first time that day she was going to have something to eat.

'It's *only one* apple. It's *only one* apple.'

The street bustled with people heading home to a dry set of clothes and a hot meal.

'God bless you ma'am. Six apples it is'.

The apples rustled in the brown paper bag as the lady, dressed in pale blue, hid beneath her umbrella.

A passer-by nudged her arm and two shillings fell to the floor.

'Not to worry ma'am, allow me'.

The magpie girl reached for the nearest apple and hid it under her shawl. She knew that the apple would no longer taste as sweet as the stallholder had promised, but at least she would eat. Life was starting to teach her the hard way that not everything in this world is as black and white as it should be.

I Want My Mummy!

Non-fiction

Inferential

Warm up Questions:

Read the title.
- Who do you think this text might be for, Key Stage 1 or 2? (Key Stage 1) Why? (It sounds quite babyish)

Read paragraph one.
- Who do you now think the text is for, infants or juniors? (Key Stage 2) Why? (it would be hard for smaller children to understand and it's quite gory)

- Who is the Egyptian god you can see on the page? (Anubis) What was he the god of? (mummification)

Main Questions:

1. Do you think Anubis believed helping the High Priest was a good thing or a bad thing? (good) Why do you think this? (he says it is a worthy goal)

2. Would the iron hook used for scraping out the brain have been long or short? (long) Draw your answer. Why did you draw it this way? (it has to go up through the nose)

3. Why do you think the cut for removing the organs was small and not large? (a large cut would spoil the body)

4. Would this have made the removal of organs easy or more difficult? (more difficult) Why? (they would have to come out through a small hole)

5. Once the body had dried out, do you think it would (a) be fragile? (yes) (b) smell? (yes, but not unpleasantly) (c) be smaller and lighter? (yes) (d) be beautiful to look at? (no)

6. Do you think the priests who mummified the pharaoh would have to be patient? (yes) Why? (the whole process took at least 70 days)

7. Why do you think grave robbers often damage mummies? (mummies are very fragile and the robbers are careless)

Essential Vocabulary:

- Can you find another word for 'dead body' in paragraph 3? (corpse)

- Highlight the word 'scrape'. Does this word suggest the removal of the brain would be quick and easy or long and difficult? (long and difficult)

- On a scale of 1 – 10, how noisy do you think this word is?

- What was the name for the special salt used for drying out a dead body? (natron)

- What word in paragraph 5 means 'more than you need'? (surplus)

- Circle a word in paragraph 7 that means 'the whole of' or 'all'. (entire)

- The prefix 're' means to do something again. Can you spot any 're' words in paragraphs 4 and 5. (remove, repack)

- With a partner, make a list of as many 're' words as you can. Show your list to the group.

Evaluative Questions:

- Why do you think Anubis, and not the writer, tells you about the mummification process? (he is meant to be addressing the reader directly) Did you like or dislike this idea? Why?

- How did the presentation of the page help you follow the set of instructions clearly? Make a list with your teacher.

- How well do you think the title goes with the text? If you could change it, what would you change it to and why?

I Want My Mummy!

Let me introduce myself. My name is Anubis and I am the ancient Egyptian god of mummification. I hear you wish to become an apprentice to the High Priest. A worthy goal indeed! But be warned my friend…succeed and the gods will smile upon you with generosity, fail and their curse will hang around your neck for all eternity.

After washing and shaving your master, you are ready to begin making your mummy. First, take an iron hook and scrape out the brain through one of the nostrils. After doing this, make a small cut on the left hand side of the corpse so that you can remove the lungs, liver, stomach and intestines. Place these to one side for later use.

With the corpse now empty, place the body into an embalming bath and pack inside and out with natron - a salt-like powder found in the desert. Do the same with the internal organs removed from the body.

Having waited forty days, remove the now dried-out body from the bath and rinse off the natron with water. Pat dry and rub the flesh with oil and wine perfumed with spices.

In order to keep its shape, the body will now need re-packing with a combination of linen, sawdust and bundles of surplus natron. This process will also need to be applied to the internal organs.
* Please note the key below so as not to mix them up!

To make your mummy appear more lifelike, first fill the nostrils with beeswax and paint a face on to the skin itself. A golden mask can be placed on top if wanted. Remember, glass eyes make beautiful replacements, as do gold-tipped finger and toe nails.

The embalming process now over, you can complete your mummy by gently wrapping him in the finest linen: first individual fingers and toes, before wrapping each limb and then finally the entire body.

It may have taken you seventy days of hard (and sometimes messy) work but your job is now done and your master is ready to be sent into the next world with the honour and the glory he deserves.

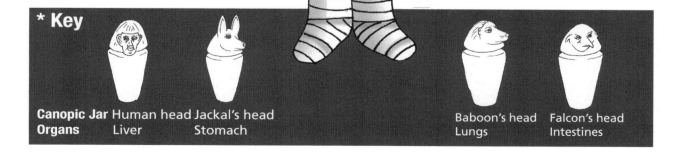

* Key

| **Canopic Jar** | Human head | Jackal's head | | Baboon's head | Falcon's head |
| **Organs** | Liver | Stomach | | Lungs | Intestines |

A Jockey's Life

Poetry

Warm up Questions:

■ On what might you see a jockey? Draw your answer.

■ What is a jockey supposed to do? (help a horse to win a race)

■ Are jockeys known for being big, strong men or being small and puny? (small and puny) Why might this be important when competing in a horse race? (they don't weigh much)

Main Questions:

1. Who do you think enjoyed their adventures the most, the writer or his brother? (the writer) Why do you think this? (he remembers it clearly)

2. How old do you think the writer was when granddad told him this poem? (a) 0- 5 years old? (b) 5-6 years old? (c) 10-11 years old? (d) 12+ years old? (b) Why? (he was riding on his granddad's shoulders but was old enough to discuss the poem)

3. Pretend you are granddad (or grandma) telling your grandchildren this poem. Practise reading the poem out loud and answer these questions:

4. Do you think the jockey believes life is easy or hard? (hard) Why? ("life ain't all honey")

5. Do you think the jockey is good at his job? (no) How do you know? (he didn't win races)

6. Is the jockey somebody who gives up easily, yes or no? (no) Why do you think this? (he keeps trying)

7. Who do you think the jockey is talking to in the poem? (his boss)

8. What do you think he is trying to say? (please don't sack me, give me another chance)

9. Why do you think granddad had to explain the poem to his grandchildren? (a) they were not very bright? (b) the poem used old words and phrases that they didn't understand? (b)

Essential Vocabulary:

■ Write the word 'cooped' onto your wipe board. Now underline the place where a chicken lives and draw one.

■ Is a chicken coop big or small, light or dark, spacious or cramped? (small, dark, cramped)

■ Why do you think grandad uses the phrase 'cooped up' before going for a walk? (that's how he feels when he's indoors)

■ Highlight the word 'stallion'. Is a stallion male or female, big and strong or small and weak? (male, big, strong)

■ Highlight the poem's punchline. How does this tell us this poem is quite old? (the jockey calls the police van the 'Black Maria')

Evaluative Questions:

■ Why did the poem 'A Jockey's Life' make granddad and the writer laugh?

■ Why do you think granddad told his grandchildren this poem?

■ Do you think the writer will tell his grandchildren this poem when he is old? Why do you think this?

A Jockey's life

He loved the outdoors.

'Being cooped up all day is only a job for us chickens', he used to say.

It was his way of telling us that we were about to get some fresh air.

During the school holidays my grandad would always take me and my brother on an adventure, either to Carr Wood or Ashworth Valley.

One summer, as I was riding high on his shoulders like a king riding a white stallion, he taught us a poem his father had taught him when he was a lad. My brother doesn't remember it any more, but I do. It went something like this…

A jockey's life ain't all honey,
Though folks put me down as a frost.
I'd be at the top today Sir,
If I'd won all the races I've lost.
Many a time I've come third…
(With three runners)
Which proves I'm always a trier.
I've rode in the Oaks and the Leger,
And also the Black Maria!

I remember turning to him, shaking my head.
'I don't get it'.

'It's easy really. But then everything's easy when you know the answers.'

I still didn't get it.

'Honey is something sweet to the taste, while frost is something you want to avoid'.

'Oh I see, so he's trying to say a jockey's life is not always sweet and that people don't put money on him to win anymore'.

'That's right, and the Oaks and the Leger are famous horse races'.

'I get it now. So the Black Maria is a horse race too?'

'No, that's the punch line. It's an old nickname for a police van.'

He laughed and after I'd thought about it for some time, I laughed too.

The North Wind Doth Blow

Narrative

Warm up Questions:

- What is a fable? (a story with a moral) Make a list of ideas with your teacher. Look at the title. Who might one of the main characters in the fable be? (the North Wind)

- If you had to describe the real North Wind, how might you do so?

strong	gentle	harsh	kind
scorching	cruel	weak	freezing

(strong, cruel, harsh, freezing)

- How might this influence the North Wind's character? (he would be unkind, selfish, unfriendly)

Main Questions:

1. Who do you think is younger, the sun or the North Wind? (the North Wind) Why do you think this? (he seems to be trying to prove himself)

2. Act out the first part of this fable with a partner. How should the sun and the North Wind speak? (gently, harshly) Why do you think this? (it goes with their characters)

3. What do you think was happening when 'the sun's smile grew wider'? (it was getting hotter)

4. As the sun began to shine, why do you think
   (a) the birds were chirping? (they felt warm)
   (b) the children were giggling? (they were laughing because the newspaper had blown away)

5. Look at the actions of the old man. What do his actions tell us about his character? Make a list with your teacher.

6. Why do you think the North Wind vanished with a 'huff and a puff'? (he was annoyed because he had lost. It also reminds us of the wolf in the three little pigs)

Essential Vocabulary:

- Highlight the word 'exhausted'. Is this word strong or weak? (strong) On a scale of 1 – 10, how tired was the North Wind? (10 at the end of the story)

- Circle the word 'coiled'. Draw a snake that is 'coiled up'.

- Why do you think the writer uses this word to describe the North Wind at this time? (the Wind was swirling round like an invisible snake)

- Put a box around the word 'glorious'. Is this word positive or negative, strong or weak? (positive and strong) What do you think this word means in this sentence? (a) very beautiful? (b) being full of glory (like a gold medal winner)? both? (a)

- Find a word in the moral box that means 'to get'. (gain) Is this word formal or informal? (formal)

- Highlight the key word in the moral box. (persuasion) What do you think it means? (a) to tell? (b) to persuade? (b)

Evaluative Questions:

- In your own words, tell a partner what the moral of this fable is.

- How do people use persuasion (a) to sell something on the TV or in supermarkets? (b) to get a friend to go to the cinema with them?

- Do you agree or disagree that this is better than using force? Why?

The North Wind Doth Blow

High above the Earth the North Wind swirled and whirled about the sun.

'Is there something I can help you with?' the sun asked politely.

'Ha! You think you're so great don't you? But I know better and I will prove it to anyone who cares to watch.'

'And how, may I ask, are you going to do that?' replied the sun, raising her eyebrows.

'See that old man down there, sitting on the park bench, reading his paper? Well, so strong am I that I will blow his coat right off his back and send it to heaven itself'.

'Be my guest,' she smiled. 'Perhaps I will wear it myself.'

And from that moment on she did not utter another word.

No sooner had the poor man turned a page than the North Wind set to work. He coiled around him like an invisible snake, whistling and wailing as he did so.

But the withered hands of the old man clung to his coat with all their strength. And no matter how hard the North Wind blew, the old man would not let go.

Exhausted, the North Wind began to calm and as he did so he looked towards the mighty sun.

Without a sound, the sun began to shine. The birds chirped up and some children giggled as they brought the old man's paper back.

Before long, the old man had stopped hugging his coat and was undoing the buttons. The sun's smile grew wider and in no time at all the old man had taken off his coat altogether and was hanging it neatly over the park bench.

With no more than a huff and a puff, the North Wind vanished, leaving the old man to read his paper in peace and enjoy the glorious sunshine that now smiled upon him.

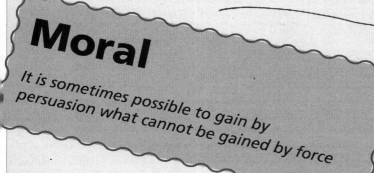

Moral

It is sometimes possible to gain by persuasion what cannot be gained by force

www.squashedtomato.com

Narrative

Warm up Questions:

- What film is being reviewed on this website? (The Quest II) What rating has this film been given? (12A) Who is the film's director? (Danny Wells)

- How long is this film? (a) just under two hours? (b) exactly two hours?   (c) just over two hours? (c)

- Who do you think is reviewing this film? (a) Danny Wells? (b) Edward Johnson?   (c) Daisy McNeil?   (d) Gemma Foster? (d)

Main Questions:

1. What genre of film do you think 'The Quest II' will be? (fantasy adventure) Make a list with your teacher why you think this.

2. Do you think this film is meant for younger or older children? (older)

3. Draw The Dark Lord of Oberon. Explain to your partner why you have drawn him like this.

4. Who do you think will win the battle of good v evil?

5. What do you think Gemma means when she writes 'the audience is blown away...' (amazed) Show your teacher.

6. Does paragraph six suggest this film is being talked about by lots of people or just a few? (lots)

7. Do you think Gemma believes this film will be a success? (yes) Why does she suggest you buy your ticket early? (to make sure you don't miss it)

Essential Vocabulary:

- Why do you think this film uses the word 'quest' rather than 'journey' in its title? (it means a search rather than just a journey)

- What do you think the 'II' means after the word 'Quest'? (it's the second in a series)

- Can you find a word in paragraph two that means the same thing? (sequel)

- How does Gemma describe the following aspects of the film?

The acting	
The plots	
The backdrops	
The lighting	
The costume	

- On a scale of 1 – 10, how strong would you describe these adjectives?

- Does the use of these strong adjectives suggest Gemma (a) likes the film? (b) loves the film? (b)

- Is a 'banquet' big or small? (big) What does this word suggest about the amount of 'thrills and spills' in this film? (there are lots of them)

Evaluative Questions:

- Out of a maximum of 5, how many squashed tomatoes do you think Gemma will award The Quest II? Draw your answer.

- Why do you think this?

- What effect do you think this review will have on the reader? Why?

- How might this affect ticket sales to this film?

- Do you think it is important to read or listen to other peoples' views on a film before going to see it? Why?

THE QUEST II (12A)

Director: *Danny Wells*
Cast: *Edward Johnson, Daisy McNeil*
Running Time: 128 minutes

A chance meeting in a second hand bookstore sees our two loveable heroes Brad and Kate set off on a journey to unlock the hidden secrets of Atlantis. However, as in most quests, all too soon they are pitted against a host of difficulties and a collection of colourful villains, including their old foe The Dark Lord of Oberon.

Facing the age-old battle of good v evil that so many of us enjoyed last year, this long-awaited sequel serves up a banquet of thrills and spills that will bring the cinema screen alive yet again.

With the biggest budget in movie history, it is not hard to see where the money has been spent. From the opening scene to the closing credits, the audience is blown away by the latest in CGI technology and special effects that make the unbelievable believable.

But this is not a film carried along by spectacular visual effects alone. Far from it! The acting is superb and the plot so exciting that at times it is hard to catch your breath. Grab your popcorn, you're in for an incredible ride!

Shot on location in New Zealand and the South Pole, the backdrops to this film are simply stunning, the lighting fantastic. The costumes and sets have been designed to perfection and all of this comes together to help transport you into the world of fantasy and spectacle with ease.

With the hype about The Quest II being sky-high, this film was in serious danger of failing to deliver. However, this action packed adventure has all the signs of being a classic and its quality is there for everyone to be amazed by.

This must see blockbuster hits your screens this Friday. Make sure you book your tickets early!

Gemma Foster

The Quest II

Narrative

Warm up Questions:

- What film is this script from? (The Quest II)

- How many scenes will we be looking at in this part of the script? (2)

- Where is each scene set? (a car park and a space station)

- Which characters are in each of these scenes? (Brad, Kate, The Dark Lord of Oberon, Chief Drone)

- How does the script writer give each actor extra notes about the lines they speak? (additional acting notes are written in square brackets [])

Main Questions:

1. Why do you think Brad is out of breath at the start of Scene 16? (he had been running away)

2. When Brad puts up his hand to Kate, do you think it was open or closed? (open) What do you think this gesture means? (wait)

3. When Kate shakes her head at the end of Scene 16, what is she really saying? (a) I can't believe The Dark Lord is alive? (b) I don't believe The Dark Lord is alive? (a)

4. Do you think Brad will eventually find a dimension key on the dead man's body? (yes) Why do you think this? (all the Dark Lord's men have one)

5. Show your teacher how The Dark Lord laughs. Why do you think the script writer describes it as being 'deep'? (it sounds frightening, implies he is strong and powerful)

6. Does the script writer suggest that the Chief Drone is more or less powerful then The Dark Lord? (less) How? (the Dark Lord is giving the orders, the drone salutes him)

Essential Vocabulary:

- Highlight the word 'rummaging' in Scene 16. Show your teacher how somebody would rummage through a desk drawer. What do you think this word means? (looking for something in a very rough and untidy manner)

- Highlight the word 'menacingly' in Scene 17. Which of the three faces below looks menacing? Draw your answer.

- Which of The Dark Lord's words are written in capitals? (NO MISTAKES!)

- Do you think the actor who plays this character should say these words (a) loudly? (b) angrily? (c) both? (c)

- Make a list with your teacher of all the words that are written in italics. (not, does) Why do you think the script writer has written these words like this? (they need to be emphasised)

Evaluative Questions:

- Do you think this film would be successful at the cinema, yes or no? Why do you think this? What rating do you think this film might be classified as? Why?

- In pairs, choose one of the scenes and act it out. Show the rest of your group.

- As you watch each performance, pretend you are the film's director. How would you help the actors improve their scene?

Film Title: The Quest II

[SCENE 16]

Setting: 2am, single dog barking, light breeze blowing litter across empty parking lot.

Brad: [out of breath] That was close.

Kate: A bit too close if you ask me. Now let's get out of here before the others arrive.

Brad: Wait! [Puts up a hand] He must have one on him somewhere!
[Begins rummaging through the dead agent's pockets]

Kate: One what? [Looking confused]

Brad: [not looking up] Part of me wants him *not* to have one, but I've got a horrible feeling about this.

Kate: [frustrated] One what?

Brad: A dimension key, what else? All The Dark Lord's men have one. It's how they jump space and time here on Earth without being detected.

Kate: And if he *does* have one, then we know he's been sent from Oberon, right?

Brad: [now checking his inside pockets] Right!

Kate: But…but that's [shaking her head] impossible. We saw The Dark Lord die with our own eyes. I blew up the tanker myself.

[CUT TO SCENE 17]

Setting: Space Station Delta 3, Mission Control Room, main computer screen shows Brad and Kate in the parking lot.

The Dark Lord of Oberon: Nothing is impossible my dear…nothing! [Deep laughter follows. He turns to his chief drone] Send in Metamorph and tell him his orders are to capture them alive. They're the only ones who know the whereabouts of the Book of Secrets and have the expertise to decode it. Do I make myself clear?

Chief Drone: Yes, master. [Nods his head once and salutes]

The Dark Lord of Oberon: Then make it so. And this time, NO MISTAKES! [Bangs his fist on a nearby computer panel and stares menacingly at the computer screen]

Campfire's Burning

Narrative

Warm up Questions:

- Read the lyrics to the song at the start of this text.

- Where do you think this scene might be set?
  Draw your answer.

- What do you think is just about to happen?
  Why do you think this?

Main Questions:

1. Do you think this scene is set in the day or at night? (night)
   Why? (there are shadows and silhouettes)

2. Look at the pictures below.

   Draw the picture that best illustrates what the 'beast' is.

3. Why do you think this?

4. Why do you think the writer refers to the fire as being 'caged'? (It is contained within a stone circle, not free to roam).

5. When the beast is 'fed', what do you think it is eating? (wood) Why? (to keep the fire alight)

6. If the 'beast' were to 'bite' somebody, what would happen to him or her? (a) they'd be scratched? (b) they'd be bitten? (c) they'd be burnt? (c)

7. What type of story do you think the storyteller is about to tell? (a ghost story)

8. Pretend you are the storyteller. How might you start your terrifying tale? Show your group. Why have you chosen to start your story in this way?

Essential Vocabulary:

- Highlight the word 'huddled'. If we all huddled together would we be very close to each other or far apart? (close to each other)

- Does this word suggest the night is warm or cold? (cold) Why? (they're huddling together to keep warm)

- The 'chill' looks for anyone who is foolish enough to 'venture away' from the fire. Underline this phrase in the text. What do you think it means? (people who go away from the fire will get cold)

- When the storyteller 'rose' to his feet, do you think he stood up slowly or quickly? (slowly) Show your teacher.

- Draw a tame cat and a wild cat. What is the difference? (a wild cat is fierce)

- Why do you think the writer uses the word 'tamed' to describe the fire? (it can be controlled)

Evaluative Questions:

- Who is the main character in this scene, the storyteller or the campfire? (the campfire) Why do you think the writer did this?

- Did you like the writer's idea of making the fire a beast that was imprisoned? Why?

- Why is it more likely the storyteller will tell a tale of horror than a comedy or love story?

Campfire's Burning!

Campfire's burning, campfire's burning.
Draw nearer, draw nearer.
Fire, fire! Fire, fire!
Draw near and be merry.

She had not asked to be tamed in this way, a caged lion longing to roam free.

But a circle of stones held her tightly in her prison and she could do little to escape.

She hissed and she crackled and she spat, ablaze with anger and fury.

But her spectators would not let her go and instead huddled around her, hypnotized by her beauty, the gold and amber ribbons in her hair flickering in the darkness.

From time to time, one of her jailers would come and feed her, not daring to step too close for fear of being bitten.

A chill watched from behind the trees for anyone foolish enough to venture away from the beast's warm glow.

An owl hooted somewhere in the shadows beyond.

It was then, and only then, as if the owl had somehow called to him, that the storyteller rose to his feet.

The beast danced with excitement.

'Let it begin. Let it begin,' she cried.

And with a deep breath and a wild look in his eyes, he did just so…

Learning Style Questionnaire

✓ Tick one or two boxes from the following ten questions. Then add up your total at the bottom of each column. This will indicate your preferred learning style.

Question	Visual 👁 👁	Auditory 👂	Kinaesthetic ✋
1. When I am learning something new I say…	demonstrate it to me. ☐	explain it to me. ☐	let me try it on my own. ☐
2. To relax I often…	watch a film or pick up a book. ☐	listen to my favourite music. ☐	take part in sports or other exercise. ☐
3. When I am having trouble spelling a word I…	visualise the word in my head. ☐	say the word aloud. ☐	put pen to paper and try writing it. ☐
4. When cooking a new dish I…	follow the instructions from the recipe book. ☐	ask a friend for some advice. ☐	don't bother with a recipe and just have a go. ☐
5.When it is important for me to remember something I…	try to make a mental picture. ☐	think back to what was said or heard. ☐	act out what I was doing. ☐
6. What distracts me when I want to learn is…	an untidy room or desk. ☐	if it is too noisy. ☐	if the temperature is too hot or cold. ☐
7. To keep up to date with the news I…	read a newspaper. ☐	listen to a news report. ☐	surf the Internet. ☐
8. When buying a new computer game I…	look at the reviews. ☐	ask a friend for some advice. ☐	test it out myself. ☐
9. What's your favourite day out?	Watching a firework display. ☐	Going to watch a band play. ☐	Going to a theme park. ☐
10. What type of party would you most like to go to?	A fancy dress party. ☐	One with lots of music and dancing. ☐	One with lots of party games. ☐
Total =	☐	☐	☐

The questionnaire shows me I am a .... learner.

Your teacher will now hand you some extra information. It contains some handy hints on how to become a better learner. Discuss these ideas with your group.

What kind of learner am I?

How did you get on with your questionnaire? Were you surprised at the result? Below are some handy hints to help you become a better learner when studying.

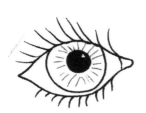 

A visual student

- Make sure your study area is neat and well organised. A messy desk = a messy mind!

- Draw pictures and diagrams about the things you are learning. Use colours and interesting designs. Make sure these are well spaced out and not too cluttered.

- Display your work in places where you will see it regularly, for example, put up a poster on your bedroom wall rather than hide it in a book.

An auditory student

- When studying, make sure it is quiet. Sometimes music can help but only if it isn't too loud. Research shows classical music is best.

- Find someone who will listen and talk to you about what you are learning. Two heads are better than one, so share your ideas freely.

- If you are on your own, then read your book out loud or listen to it on a CD.

A kinaesthetic student

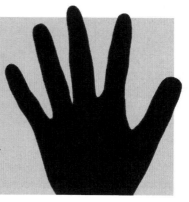

- Move while you learn – BE ACTIVE. Movement stimulates memory!

- Imagine yourself doing whatever it is you are learning. Acting things out is a great way to remember something!

- Build a model of whatever you are learning about and attach labels to it.

REMEMBER
The best students use all three methods of study.
Experiment to see which type of student you are and what things help you learn.
Remember, people change over time, so your learning style might change too!

Title and Genre of text:

How to use a library

Genre

Warm up Questions:

- What book are you reading at the moment? Is this book meant to:
  make you laugh? make you cry?
  scare you? keep you in suspense?
  How does it do this?

- After listening to the other group members talk about the books they are reading, which one do you think would be most like yours? Why do you think this?

- Can you think of a way a library or bookshop might group different types of books together?

Main Questions:

Initial Activity:

The initial part of this lesson can be done as a whole group activity. Blow up the table on page 75. Cut out and laminate each 'card'. Shuffle them and hand one card from each section to a member of the group. You can then guide the group, as well as discuss reasons for their decision-making, as they try to help Pierre put his genre poster back together again.

Follow Up Questions:

1. Draw another character you might find in the horror genre. Show your group. Do they agree or disagree with you?

2. Draw a piece of technology you might find in the science fiction genre. Describe it to your group.

3. Which genre is usually set in the past (western) and future (Sci-fi)? Why?

4. In pairs, act out a scene from one of the books in Pierre's poster. Show your group. Can they guess which book you are trying to recreate? What clues helped them make their decision?

Essential Vocabulary:

- What do you think the word 'genre' means? (a) a kind of book or film? (b) a type of place where you can read books? (a) Do you think the word 'genre' is an English word, yes or no? (no) Why? (it is not pronounced in an English way)

- Copy the heading of each genre onto your wipe board. How has Pierre used different fonts to help convey each genre? Do you think this is effective? How?

- Libraries often put a symbol for each genre on the 'spine' of a book. Point to the following: your own spine; the spine of a book.

- Below are six symbols that a library might use for each genre in Pierre's poster*

 Romance   Sci-Fi

 Horror   Western

 Comedy   Mystery

Which one would you put on the spine of each of the books in Pierre's poster? Why?

- Write down the author of each book in Pierre's poster. What do you notice? (the names are made up to reflect the title of the book)

* These symbpls are on the CD

Evaluative Questions:

Your teacher will now show you some real books from your class or school library.

- Which genre do you think each book should be classified as?

- Why do you think this?

- Are some books hard to classify? Why?

- Which genre do you prefer to read? Why?

- Films also use genre in the same way that books do. With your teacher, make a list of films you have seen this year. What genre do you think they might be?

Genre

Libraries and bookstores often group fictional books together according to their genre. This allows their customers to find a particular book more easily.

This poster looks at six genres. However, Pierre has mixed up the different sections by mistake. Can you help him sort them out before his boss finds out?

Front Cover	Character	Setting	Quote	Genre
The Grave Shift By A. Vein			*"Not knowing that he'd tucked his shirt into his underpants, James set off to school. Little did he realize but this was going to turn out to be an extremely bad day."*	**SCI-FI**
Sweet Valley High Val N. Tine		Sweet Valley High	*"Inspector Doyle took off his gloves and walked briskly into the study. There, slumped over his desk with a knife in his back, was the body of Charles Toffsbury."*	**WESTERN**
Sitting Bull Rides Again By G. Upp			*"'Sheriff, you gotta come quick! Quick Draw McGraw's just ridden into town and people are mighty scared.' Without another word, he picked up his revolver and left…"*	**Mystery**
Return to Planet Dread By I. Podd			*"'Computer, exactly how long have we got?' Three minutes, twenty four seconds and counting. There was nothing more he could do. Captain Teller began running to the escape pod."*	**Romance**
Murder at the Manor Hans Cuft		JAIL SHERIFF	*"…and as she gazed into his watery eyes, her heart began to race. Could Troy, the captain of the football team, really fall for a computer geek like her?"*	**COMEDY**
There's a leaf in my Soup Teresa Green			*"A blood-curdling scream pierced the air. Then… nothing! Moments later, a bat flew silently from the castle window and vanished into the dead of night."*	**HORROR**

Title and Genre of text:

How to use a Contents and Index page

Pirates I

Warm up Questions:

- In which type of book would you usually find Contents and Index pages? (non-fiction)

- Whereabouts in a book would you find each of these pages? (Contents at the beginning, Index at the end) What does each of these pages help us to do? (find out where different topics are)

- Which page is set out numerically (Contents) and which is alphabetical (Index)? What do the numbers mean after each subject? (page numbers)

Main Questions:

Contents Page

1. On which pages would you find the following?
   - What pirates ate while at sea (28)
   - Whether there were any female pirates (20)
   - A useful website address about pirates (40)

Index Page

2. On which pages might you find the following information?
   - What salt was used for on board a pirate ship? (25, 29)
   - What different designs were used for The Jolly Roger? (15)
   - How pirates have been shown on film at the cinema? (35)
   - How rats plagued the lives of pirates? (25, 29)

3. Do you think the following pirates were real or not? Use both pages to help you.
   (Jack Rackham, Blackbeard and Jean Bart were real)

   | Jack Rackham | Blackbeard | Long John Silver |
   | Jean Bart | Captain Hook | |

4. Which of these pirates was a woman? (Jean Bart)

Essential Vocabulary:

- Circle an example of the following symbol: &. What does this symbol represent? (and)

- Highlight the word 'imprisonment'. Write it onto your wipe board.

- Can you spot another word hidden inside it? Underline your answer. (prison)

- What do you think the word 'imprisonment' means?

- Write the word 'literature' onto your wipe board.

- Which lesson do you do in class that sounds like this word? (literacy)

- How do you think this lesson got its name?

- Highlight the word 'piracy'. Explain to a partner what you think this word means. (it's what a pirate does)

- Why is downloading music and films from the internet without paying sometimes described as piracy?

Evaluative Questions:

- Your teacher will now show you some more Contents and Index pages found in other non-fiction books in your school or class library.

- Using only the Contents and Index pages to help you:
  Which book would you most likely pick up and read? Why?
  Which book would you least likely pick up and read? Why?

- Do other members of the group agree or disagree with you?

- Is it fair to judge a book on how its Contents and Index pages look?

Pirates

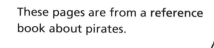

The Contents Page is found towards the front of the book. It tells us what chapters are in the book, together with the page numbers they are on.

The Index is found at the back of the book. It lists specific information located in the book in alphabetical order, and tells us on which page to find it.

Both the Contents Page and Index help us to find information fast when researching a topic.

These pages are from a reference book about pirates.

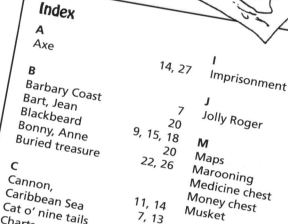

Contents Page

3

Index

41

Title and Genre of text:

How to use a Glossary

Pirates II

Warm up Questions:

- In what type of book would you find a glossary? (non-fiction)

- Whereabouts in a book would you find a glossary? (at the end) On what page would you find this glossary? (38)

- How are the words in a glossary organized? (alphabetically)

Main Questions:

1. What was the name of a pirate who attacked Spanish ships in the 1600s? (buccaneer)

2. What material was a doubloon made from? (gold)

3. What happened to a pirate if he got scurvy? (he would get bleeding gums and spots) How could pirates stop themselves from getting scurvy? (by eating fruit and vegetables which provided vitamin C)

4. From where would criminals be hanged? (from a gallows) Where might their dead bodies be displayed? (on a gibbet) Why? (to discourage other criminals)

5. Draw a Cat o' nine tails. What was this used for? (punishing sailors)

6. After reading this glossary, do you think pirate life was easy or difficult, peaceful or violent? (difficult and violent)

7. What clues on the page suggest this? Make a list with your teacher.

Essential Vocabulary:

- Highlight the word 'becalmed'. Copy it onto your wipe board. There is another word hidden inside this word. Can you underline it? (calm)

- Draw a 'becalmed' sea.

- Why was this bad for a pirate? (because his ship couldn't go anywhere)

- Circle the word 'unravelling'.

- Do you think this is a positive or negative word? (negative) Why? (it begins with 'un')

- If you had to unravel some string, how would you do it? Show your teacher.

- Why would a 'waggoner' be useful to a pirate? (it was a book of sea maps)

- Is this a modern or old-fashioned word? (old-fashioned)

- Why do you think we no longer use this word? (Sailors use modern technology to locate their position at sea - waggoners are no longer used)

Evaluative Questions:

- With a partner write a definition of what a glossary is. Use your own words.

- Compare your definition with those of other group members.

- Why do you think glossaries appear at the back of the book?

- What helped you find the word or phrase you were looking for more quickly? List two things.

- What do you like or dislike about this page? How would you improve it?

Pirates

A glossary is a bit like a mini-dictionary. It is an alphabetical list of specific words and phrases used in a book, together with their meanings.

Becalmed - when a sailing ship cannot move because there is no wind.

Buccaneer - a pirate who attacked Spanish ships in the West Indies and Central America during the 1600s.

Cat o' nine tails - a whip used to punish sailors, made by unravelling a piece of rope. A knot was often tied at the end of each strand to make the punishment more painful.

Chain shot - a weapon made up of two metal balls chained together. It was shot from a cannon in order to destroy a ship's rigging, masts and sails.

Colours - the flags flown by a ship.

Crow's nest - a small platform high up on a mast where a lookout would keep watch for enemy ships.

Cutlass - a short sword with a broad blade. A popular weapon when fighting, as it rarely got caught up in rigging.

Doubloon - a gold Spanish coin worth sixteen pieces of eight.

Galleon - a large sailing ship with three or more masts used between the 1500s and 1700s.

Gallows - the wooden frame used to hang criminals.

Gibbet - a wooden frame used to display the dead bodies of criminals as a warning to others.

Grappling iron - a metal hook that was thrown onto an enemy ship in order to pull it closer and make boarding easier.

Log book - the book in which the ship's voyage was recorded.

Maroon - to leave someone on a remote island – a common pirate punishment.

Rigging - the ropes that support a ship's sails and masts.

Scurvy - a disease, caused by a lack of vitamin C, which brought bleeding gums and spots. This vitamin is found in fruit (especially citrus) and vegetables.

Waggoner - A pirate term for a book of sea charts and maps.

38

Title and Genre of text:

How to use a Dictionary

Anyone for T?

Warm up Questions:

- Look at the following words:
  patience (3rd)   mayhem (2nd)   courageous (1st)
  glee (2nd)   gasp (2nd)   monstrous (3rd)

- Where would you find them in your dictionary, in the 1st, 2nd, 3rd or 4th quarter?

- In which quarter do you think you would find the letter 'T'? (4th)

- Look up these words in your own dictionary. Were you correct? Can you place these words in alphabetical order?

Main Questions:

1. Draw a river 'teeming' with fish. Now draw a picture where it is 'teeming' with rain. What do you think this word means? (raining very hard) Is the word 'teem' a modern or old word? (old)

2. Find the word that means 'to stand or move unsteadily'. (teeter) Show your teacher what this word means.

3. If somebody is 'teetotal', how often do they drink alcohol? (a) every night?   (b) once a week? (c) every now and again? d) never? (d)

4. Where might you find the material 'Teflon'? (inside a saucepan) Draw your answer.

5. How old might you be when you 'teethe'? (6 months) Can you spot another word at the start of 'teethe' that gives us a clue about what this word means? (teeth) Underline it.

6. How old might you be if you are in your 'teens'? (between 13 and 19) Is this phrase formal or informal?

Essential Vocabulary:

- Highlight the spelling pattern 'tele'. Is 'tele' a prefix or a suffix? (prefix)

- Where do we get this prefix from, the Greeks, the Romans or the Victorians? (the Greeks)

- What does the prefix 'tele' mean? (far)

- Look at the following 'tele' words:
  telephone   telescope   television

- In pairs, write down your own definition for one of these on to your wipe board.

- Now check it. Were you correct?

- Which two of these characters might be telepathic? (alien and wizard) Why? Draw your answer.

- The word 'teleport' is not on your dictionary page. If an alien 'teleported' down to Earth, what do you think he would be doing? (he would be transported without using a vehicle)

- Put a star on this dictionary page where you would put the word 'teleport'.

Evaluative Questions:

- Do you think the alphabet down the right hand side of the page is useful? How?

- How else does the writer help the reader find the word they are looking for? (the words are in alphabetical order and bold type)

- Did you find this page easy to use? Explain why or why not. How would you improve this page?

- Find the T page in your own dictionary. Compare the two pages.

- Which page do you like best? Why?

Tt

teem verb **(teems, teeming, teemed)**
be full of something. The river was teeming with fish. *(from Old English)*

teem verb **(teems, teeming, teemed)**
rain very hard; pour.

teen suffix
a form of 'ten' added to numbers from three to nine to form thirteen to nineteen.

teen adjective & noun **(teens)**
(informal) a teenager.

teenage adjective
to do with teenagers.

teenaged adjective
in your teens.

teenager noun **(teenagers)**
person in his or her teens.

teens plural noun
the time of life between 13 and 19 years of age.

tee-shirt noun
tee-shirts, a tee-shirt

teeter verb **(teeters, teetering, teetered)**
stand or move unsteadily. *(from Old Norse)*

teethe verb **(teethes, teething, teethed)**
(said about a baby) have its first teeth beginning to grow through the gums.

teetotal adjective
never drinking alcohol.

Teflon noun (trademark)
a type of plastic used as non-stick coating for pans.

tele- prefix
far; at a distance (as in telescope). *(from Greek)*

telecommunications plural noun
communications over a long distance, e.g. by telephone, telegraph, radio or television.

telegram noun **(telegrams)**
a message sent by telegraph.

telegraph noun
a way of sending messages by using electric current along wires or by radio.

telepathy (say til-ep-ath-ee) noun
communication of thoughts from one person's mind to another without speaking, writing, or gestures. telepathic adjective *(from tele-+ Greek pathos = feeling)*

telephone noun **(telephones)**
a device or system using electric wires or radio etc. to enable one person to speak to another who is some distance away

telephone verb **(telephones, telephoning, telephoned)**
speak to a person on the telephone.
(from tele- + Greek phone = sound, voice)

telephonist (say til-ef-on-ist) noun
a telephonist is a person who operates a telephone switchboard.

telescope noun **(telescopes)**
an instrument using lenses to magnify distant objects. telescopic adjective

telescope verb **(telescopes, telescoping, telescoped)**
make or become shorter by sliding overlapping sections into each other.
(from tele- + Greek skopein = look at)

teletext noun
a system for displaying news and information on a television screen.

televise verb **(televises, televising, televised)**
broadcast something by television. (from television)

television noun **(televisions)**
1 a system using radio waves to reproduce a view of scenes, events or plays etc. on a screen.
2 an apparatus for receiving these pictures.

telex noun **(telexes)**
a system for sending printed messages by telegraphy; a message sent by this system.

Title and Genre of text:

How to use a Thesaurus

Avalanche!

Warm up Questions:

Read Luke's story

- Which year group do you think Luke is in: Y3, Y4, Y5 or Y6?

- With your teacher, make a list of words that suggest this.

- Highlight them in Luke's story.

- What does Luke's teacher think of his story? (she likes it, but thinks he can make improvements)

- Do you agree or disagree? Why?

- If you wanted to help Luke improve his choice of words, which book should you look at? (a thesaurus)

- Go and get one!

Main Questions:

Having asked the warm up questions to help lead into why we use a thesaurus, the main focus of this lesson lies in the teacher developing the effective use of the thesaurus itself. This activity will enable the children to see the value of using a thesaurus in a realistic and practical setting.

However, it is important to note that once the group as a whole has been guided to the correct section of the thesaurus, individuals are encouraged to choose their own word from the selection provided. Discussion can then be elicited on a group level as to the meaning and relevance of particular synonyms. This will give individuals the opportunity to take control of the decision-making process, as well as giving them ownership of the final draft copy they have helped Luke to write.

Essential Vocabulary:

- Circle the phrase 'I'm sitting on the edge of my seat!'

- Do you think this phrase is positive or negative? (positive)

- What do you think Luke's teacher means when she writes this? (a) she is uncomfortable? (b) she is bored? (c) she is very excited? (c)

- Show your teacher how you would look if you were 'sitting on the edge of your seat' while watching a film.

- Why do you think Luke chooses to describe the avalanche as (a) a wall of snow and ice? (it was like a wall you couldn't pass through) (b) like a herd of angry white horses? (it was moving fast)

- Was this 'wall' moving fast or slowly, loudly or quietly, with force or without force? (fast, loudly, with force)

- Which word tells us this? (crashing)

Evaluative Questions:

- Do you agree or disagree with Luke's teacher that this was a 'great' first draft? Why?

- How have you helped Luke improve his story? Describe the process.

- If you were reading this story for the first time, which year group would you now think Luke was in? Y3, Y4, Y5 or Y6? Why?

- Imagine you are Luke's teacher reading his second draft. What would you write in his English book? Write it down and show your teacher.

- Now publish Luke's final draft on the computer.

Avalanche!

Tuesday 4th June

By Luke Gibson

Scott put a finger to his cold lips.

'Listen', he said. 'Can you hear that?'

A small rumbling sound had started to growl in the distance.

All they could do was stand and look as a big wall of snow and ice came crashing down the mountainside towards them like a herd of angry white horses.

Both Scott and Daniel knew that it was impossible to out-run an avalanche. Scared, they began looking around for some hope. Suddenly, out of the corner of his eye, Scott saw something. There, among the tall pine trees, was a small cave.

'Quick!' said Scott. 'It's our only hope'.

Teacher's comments

What a great first draft Luke. I'm sitting on the edge of my seat! However, I think you could make it even better by using some more descriptive words. A thesaurus will help you find the stronger words you need. You can then publish your final draft on the computer

Good Work

Notes

Reading Explorers - A Guided Skills-Based Journey - **Year 5**

Notes

About the author of this book

John Murray

John Murray is a recognised specialist in developing children's reading and listening skills through interactive and kinaesthetic approaches.

Since graduating from the University of North Wales in 1997, with a Bachelor of Education degree in English and Communication, John has taught in a wide variety of schools and situations. His experience includes teaching pupils with complex language difficulties and in communities where English is not the first language. Such challenging experiences have inspired John to create innovative new approaches to the teaching and learning of Literacy; developing techniques, ideas and methods that benefit all in the classroom.

Having created the best selling *Reading Explorers* series – highly regarded in schools across Britain and sold worldwide, he balances his teaching with his work as an independent writer and lectures on how to develop key literacy skills in leading colleges and universities. He also provides both internal and external training courses for schools.

For more information regarding resources and training from John Murray visit: **www.johnmurraycpd.co.uk**